Revolution Without the R

Helping Our Newest Generations Turn Revolution into Evolution and Change US Politics Forever

MICHAEL MARR

Over 40 years of research on explaining and forecasting political instability led me to the conclusion that our nation's insurrection on January 6, 2021, was predictable. Unfortunately, the one certainty we have is that our nation will probably experience more unrest unless we commit to improving trust in government and decrease the polarization and anxiety driving us toward ever deeper spirals of conflict. Michael Marr's work in conflict management and helping people more easily discuss political differences points us toward ways to lower our national anger with each other. Forming coalitions of like-minded citizens to work towards a better democracy, especially for our youngest voting generations, is an essential steppingstone towards returning our nation to normalcy and away from a greater conflict.

Jack A. Goldstone, Hazel Professor of Public Policy, George Mason University and author of *Revolutions: A Very Short Introduction*

Regardless of best intentions, the moment our emotions are hijacked is the moment we wish we could take back the words that created a divide. 'Revolution Without the R' is the practical learning guide to transform those moments for healing and meaningful connections.

Sheila Keitel, Organizational Development, Change Management Specialist

I've been partnering with companies and executive leaders for 15 years to help strengthen employee retention and improve individual and company performance. I had the pleasure of working with Mike while I helped him certify for a talent optimization platform. It was apparent that Michael had a natural intuitiveness and passion to help others, which comes across as he is facilitating and training others. I appreciate that he has now created learning guides and content to help address one of our primary needs - how to better handle conflict – a critical skill needed to successfully navigate today's world.

Dr. Lori Wieters, Owner/Operator at Purposeful Leadership Consulting and Chief Collaboration Officer at Wi2 Co-Lab

Revolution Without the R
Helping Our Newest Generations Turn Revolution into Evolution and Change US Politics Forever

eBook ISBN: 978-1-962570-15-2
Paperback ISBN: 978-1-962570-16-9
Hardcover ISBN: 978-1-962570-18-3
Ingram Spark ISBN: 978-1-962570-17-6
Library of Congress Control Number: 2023919015
Printed in the United States of America

Interior Design: Marigold2k
Editing: Bethany Good, https://goodwritingco.com
Published By: Spotlight Publishing House
https://spotlightpublishinghouse.com

Revolution Without the

Helping Our Newest Generations Turn Revolution into Evolution and Change US Politics Forever

MICHAEL MARR

Goodyear, Arizona

Contents

Introduction

As Stephen Ayres walked from the White House where the January 6th "Save America" rally was ending and migrated towards the Capitol, his mind occupied a space most of us can't relate to.

His pre-rally social media was dark and filled with foreshadowing. One of his tweets offered the best clue of events to come on January 6th, "Time for us to start standing up to tyranny!"

As Ayres entered the field near the Capitol, he was joined by others who felt it was their patriotic duty to protest the 2020 election results. He wandered around the Capitol grounds until commotion near the main entrance to the Capitol caught his eye. It was 2:03 pm, and protest members had broken through the police barrier and now had an unencumbered path to get inside the Capitol.

You know the rest of this tragic story. In the wake of this manufactured disaster, there were 7 dead, 138 police officers injured, and a flesh wound for one of the oldest democratic nations in the world.

Like you, I watched in horror as the violence and mayhem were unleashed that day at the Capitol. That noise you probably heard as you watched the news that night was the collective gasp of 330 million people in the United States asking, "How the $#!% could something like that happen in our country?"

Experts in social psychology state that most protestors do not enjoy the type of unrest and medieval combat we witnessed on January 6th. In fact, most protests are peaceful. Yet extensive research shows that enough fear and shared frustration against a perceived enemy can create a dangerous cocktail of collective human behavior when you bring them together, and sometimes, there are just enough elements in this cocktail to produce violent reactions. On January 6th, Ayres and others had found their tipping point.[1]

By all accounts, Ayres was an ordinary person, the guy living next door. Ayres was not a member of the Oath Keepers, the 3%, or any other extremist group. His life was, by all accounts, relatively settled. He was a family man and a supervisor at a cabinet company in Ohio. Yet somehow, he was radicalized into believing that our democracy was under attack and our election had been stolen.

Could the insurrection have been avoided? Probably. But the absence of such a threat on the Capitol caused a sense of complacency among government officials. The warning signs were not taken seriously until it was too late.

Studies show plenty of warning alarms from the post-election rage that went largely ignored. Twitter's[2] internal security staff begged upper management to adopt a stricter moderation policy and not mobilizing the National Guard before the rally to handle the crowd surge were both missed opportunities.[3]

Yet I want to focus on another helpful tool you've probably never heard of, which may have acted as an early warning system for our nation's leaders before the insurrection: Revolution Science.

---

1 Frank, Jerome D. *Sanity and survival in the Nuclear Age: Psychological Aspects of war and peace.* Random House, 1987.

2 As of this publication, Twitter is now known as "X." For continuity, we will call it Twitter throughout the book.

3 Lima, Cristiano. "Analysis | Jan. 6 Panel Spotlights Twitter's Role in Insurrection." The Washington Post, July 13, 2022. https://www.washingtonpost.com/politics/2022/07/13/jan-6-panel-spotlights-twitter-role-insurrection/.

Many years ago, I began my journey as a Revolution Analyst after reading books from authors Ted Gurr, Barbara Walter, Jack A. Goldstone, and Erica Chenoweth. Their research paved the way to understand what common factors are evident before a country evolves into a revolution or other type of uprising. Equally important is the data that aids us in comprehending which warning signs can predict future uprisings.

Revolution Science studies data from thousands of past uprisings worldwide and attempts to predict where uprisings may occur next. This data helps them determine why some uprisings, like the Russian Revolution in 1917, were successful and others, like the Arab Spring in 2010, fizzled out.

How does Revolution Science predict where these uprisings will occur in the world? Is there a secret machine hidden deep in the Patagonia jungle controlled by a group of Black Ops militants who know exactly where the next revolution will occur?

Well, not exactly, sorry. (Although it would make a great Netflix thriller or our next big conspiracy theory, don't you think?)

In reality, revolutions, civil wars, and uprisings are like tornados, unpredictable to a certain degree, yet when enough elements are present, they almost always occur with volatile energy and destructive power.

The U.S. government helped to contribute to the field of Revolution Science when they sponsored the Political Instability Task Force and a group of professors to examine global data from 1995 to 2003. Their analysis helps us understand which variables were most common in a regime change so we could understand what democracies and autocracies are vulnerable to some type of uprising.[4]

---

4 "Political Instability Task Force." Wikipedia, August 19, 2022. https://en.wikipedia.org/wiki/Political_Instability_Task_Force#:~:text=The%20

Gurr and other authors who studied rebellions discovered that civil wars and revolutions also leave clues before they occur, like increased distrust of a government, the growing economic disparity between citizens, and sometimes being closely linked to other events you probably wouldn't associate with political instability, like pandemics and rising infant mortality rates within a country.

I know what you're asking, so according to Revolution Science, could a civil war, coup, revolution, or something like "The Troubles," a sustained nationalist conflict that occurred in Northern Ireland from 1968-1998, occur in the United States?

After the insurrection, I put this historical data to the test.

The short answer is if the Vice-President of the most powerful country in the world must hide in an underground parking garage protected by his security detail while thousands of protestors seek to hang him with a homemade guillotine during an insurrection…then we might be closer to some sort of serious uprising than what we think.

In this book, you'll learn some other surprising revelations about uprisings.

Spoiler Alert: You would think extremists would be the most likely group associated with a future sustained uprising in the United States, but historical data from previous conflicts says otherwise. Although vocal and loud, the insurrectionists who attacked the Capitol do not represent the largest coalition of disillusioned citizens in the United States.

Uprisings are many times a grassroots, class-based movement created by a large collective group of people dissatisfied with the government.

PITF%20first%20identified%20over,changes%2C%20and%20genocides%20and%20politicides.

I think the January 6th insurrection will pale in comparison to our next revolution, which may be fueled by the widening gap of the 'haves' and 'have nots', as well as the alarming amount of younger people leaving the Republican and Democratic parties.

So, according to the data, this supermajority of citizens who force change, hopefully peacefully, may include *you and I.*

In the United States, this coalition has yet to be formed, yet some surprising numbers are beginning to show their demographic makeup.

One segment of this coalition are those citizens who now identify themselves as "Independents," which was only 31% of voters in 2004, yet has swelled to a whopping 49% in 2023.[5] This alliance has resulted in fewer people who call themselves Republican or Democrat and should send shivers down these party leaders as they watch their influence fade.

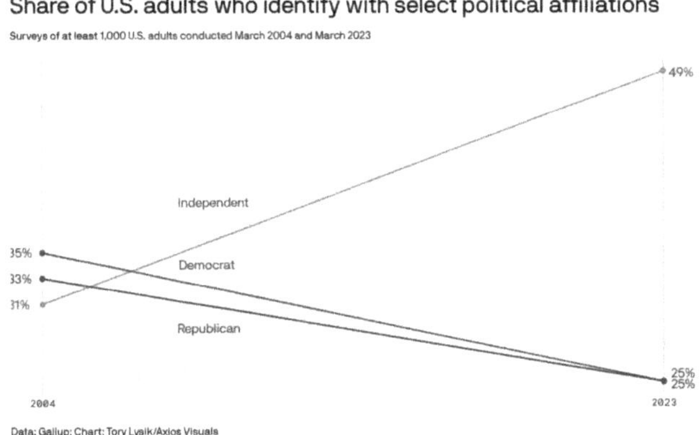

5 Mike Allen, "Record Number of Americans Say They're Politically Independent - Axios," Axios, accessed August 23, 2023, https://www.axios.com/2023/04/17/poll-americans-independent-republican-democrat.

Jeffrey M. Jones writes the likely increase in this tilt away from the Republican and Democratic parties is, "the disillusionment with the political system, U.S. institutions, and the two parties, which are seen as ineffectual, too political and too extreme.[6]" Does that sound like you?

Another worrisome sign of potential political disorder is the growing rage of the middle class, the largest group of citizens in the United States. This widening gap between the "haves" and the "have nots" is growing at an alarming rate and is one of the factors commonly seen in an uprising.[7] Indeed, author Ted Gurr writes that "over the long run of human history…a decline of a social group has probably been a more common source of collective violence.".

This widening gap was on full display during the pandemic. The middle class watched as billionaires and the top 1% grew their wealth exponentially and took rocket ships into space while they struggled to buy eggs at the grocery store and wrestled with sky-high rent increases.[8]

Another group of disillusioned citizens includes minorities and women. We saw this discontent explode in the summer of 2020 after the George Floyd killing and large groups of people who voiced their grievances after the Supreme Court decision overturning Roe V. Wade.

---

6 Allen, Axios

7 Rakesh Kochhar and Stella Sechopoulos, "How the American Middle Class Has Changed in the Past Five Decades," Pew Research Center, April 21, 2022, https://www.pewresearch.org/short-reads/2022/04/20/how-the-american-middle-class-has-changed-in-the-past-five-decades/.

8 Jessica Dickler, "Amid Inflation, More Middle-Class Americans Struggle to Make Ends Meet," CNBC, January 18, 2023, https://www.cnbc.com/2023/01/18/amid-inflation-more-middle-class-americans-struggle-to-make-ends-meet.html#:~:text=The%20middle%20class%20is%20shrinking&text=As%20is%20often%20cited%2C%20the,years%20earlier%2C%20according%20to%20Pew.

I believe this "coalition of the disillusioned" also includes our youngest generation of voters who are leaving the Republican and Democratic parties in record numbers[9] due to burdening college debt, out-of-reach housing costs, and the weight of climate change.

My interviews with our newest voting generations revealed that many feel these problems were caused by previous generations. Their perception that they may have nothing to lose could be a large factor in shaping the outcome of some type of uprising.[10]

The newest factor that adds to the growing amount of checkmarks we see in rebellions wasn't around when early pioneers were discussing rebellion. Yet, it's an effective tool for those who seek to divide us: the chilling effect biased media has on influencing the political landscape in the US.

Feel free to call me an alarmist, but I believe analysts who study a country's susceptibility to instability have severely underestimated the effects that prolonged social media and biased news have on people like Stephen Ayres.

You'll read in my chapter titled "Emojis Against Reality" just how politicians and technology platforms have supercharged the influence code in our brains and used it as a weapon to help radicalize people.

One of my mentors who influenced me to write about revolution science was Barbara F. Walter. She put it best in her book "How Civil Wars Start: And How to Stop Them," when she said, "I know the

9 "Young People's Ambivalent Relationship with Political Parties," Circle at Tufts, October 24, 2018, https://circle.tufts.edu/latest-research/young-peoples-ambivalent-relationship-political-parties.

10 J. E. SPENCE, Book Reviews, Community Development Journal, Volume 7, Issue 3, October 1972, Pages 199–200, https://doi.org/10.1093/cdj/7.3.199

signs that people miss. And I can see those signs emerging here at a surprisingly fast rate.[11]"

Yet my book isn't focused on how to store grains, eggs, and building a bunker waiting for some type of uprising to occur. My book isn't about how to get back at the "other side" for their mean tweets or even why many totally disregard talking politics at all.

The book is about hope.

And it starts with you, yes, you.

I believe the road to normalcy in our country doesn't begin with others. It begins with looking at your responses to the daily bombardment of data you see covered on how broken our country is and reshaping your response to fit reality.

You know that Uncle who drives you crazy at Thanksgiving dinner because he loves to tell you the politician you voted for is single-handedly destroying the country?

We're going to show how to mentally shield yourself from his nonsense and offer scientific reasons why you should cut him a little slack. In my chapter titled "MAGA Hats and Snowflakes," we'll teach you how to manage this "amygdala hijack" and better control these reactions.

The strategies we'll discuss aren't just self-help hacks to help you think better about your world, but real tools like our "Angry Uncle Chatbot" to practice simple conflict management conversations taught by the very best in the industry so you can finally enjoy your Thanksgiving dinner and any other conflict that comes your way. (Pass the mashed potatoes, please.)

---

[11] Walter, Barbara F, *How Civil Wars Start: And How to Stop Them*. London, UK: Penguin Books, 2023.

I know at times you feel our country may never return to normalcy, but in the pages ahead, you'll also read how other countries like South Africa, Northern Ireland, and Somalia migrated their way out of hate and back to some form of civility, peace, and understanding after brutal periods when neighbors fought neighbors, and peace seemed like a distant planet.

Finally, and perhaps most importantly, you'll get to read fresh perspectives from my interviews with our newest generation of voters and see what they want from a future democracy.

When I asked our youngest voters who controlled the power in the United States, they almost unanimously answered with some version of "Politicians influenced by larger corporations."

Their voice was clear in my interviews: they don't just want "our hope" for a better generation. They want us to listen and care about what they want from a new democracy.

I believe their thoughts echo the same as most of you reading this book, and for good reasons.

Baratunde Thurston, Harvard Graduate and host of the wonderful podcast "How To Citizen," reveals, "When you turn on the news or read about it online, most of the messages we receive is how broken the world is, how divided we are. You also hear headlines that democracy is in crisis, democracy is fragile, and how powerless we are to fix it."

Yet Baratunde emphasizes that the message is incomplete. He states, "You aren't hearing about all the work being done to mend it."

In my book, you'll read about people who are fighting to make that happen, about our youth who are begging us to improve democracy, and about simple ways you can wrestle that power away from the small majority of people who have weaponized democracy and reclaim it as a collective nation.

You'll also read about what you can do.

The direction in which our democracy tilts rests in our hands. Many believe citizens do not have the power to control the trajectory of our country. Yet by the end of the book, I hope when I ask who has the power in the United States, you'll believe, "all of us."

Let's get started on this journey of evolution and learning.

Raise your hand if you've been told by friends that our nation has never been divided. Wow - that's a lot of hands!

Our first chapter delves into thought distortions and the dismantling of the artificial barriers we perceive as dividing us.

Before jumping into the next chapter, I urge you to visit our linktree site: https://linktr.ee/evolutionrevolutionnow and take a quick quiz titled "The Perception Gap." This quiz will shed light on those thought distortions you may have and the significance they have on both your personal well-being and the trajectory of our nation.

Welcome to the evolution that will reshape and permanently influence U.S. politics for yourself and future generations.

Chapter 1

Tornados and Insurrections: The Mike Pence Story

Summer is a magical time for a kid growing up in the Midwest.

As spring emerges, the cold, gray, agonizing days of being stuck inside give way to the promise of warm weather made for playing outside until streetlights come on and Mother beckons you home.

Summer carries with it unique aromas and cherished memories: the fragrance of just-mowed grass, the alluring aroma of barbeque chicken your father would prepare on Sundays, and the recollection of your dog enthusiastically licking the chocolate syrup you accidentally spilled on a corner of your shirt during the 4th of July neighborhood picnic.

But in the Midwest, summer is also the time for tornados.

Denise remembers the tornado that appeared uninvited on her doorstep in 1981.

Denise's mom had left her California life in Haight-Ashbury for Churubusco, Indiana, exchanging life in a commune for cows, cattle, and the slower pace a farm offers.

Denise remembers scary phenomena like earthquakes when she lived in California, but thankfully, nothing like that ever happened in her safe town of Churubusco, Indiana.

"Busko," as the locals call it, is known for its charm and friendly people. Like most Midwestern towns, the town enjoys its share of lore and even has a favorite mascot. Busko was no different. The town's endearing "Oscar the Turtle" reportedly haunted nearby Fulk's lake. The town's Turtle Days, a favorite with residents, returned yearly with parades honoring Veterans, carnival rides, a junior beauty pageant, and plenty of snow cones that acted as rocket fuel for the kids.

For Denise and her friends, it was a time to show off the ribbons you won for having the prize cow and staying out way too late.

June 9th, 1981 was pretty much like any other day, except that Denise and her mom were visiting Ft. Wayne, a larger city about 16 miles northwest of the town.

When the skies darkened that day, Denise's mother tuned her car's am radio to hear the weather forecast. There was no satellite radio or Doppler radar back then, just "spotters" that the county counted on to watch for funnel clouds that could eventually evolve into tornados.

Tornados are one of the deadliest natural disasters in the United States, boasting more than any other country in the world. On average, 1,200 of these wind bombs appear, and on June 9th, 1981, Denise's town of Churubusco sat right in the path of an angry, oncoming F-4 tornado.

Denise remembers the skies getting dark and quickly getting hurried into the car. "I remember hearing something on the AM radio that a tornado was coming and my mom driving like a bat out of hell racing to get home." She recalls that it seemed like such a long ride home, and there wasn't anyone on the streets that she found odd.

On the way home, Denise did what any other typical child might do: look for the tornado. She remembers her mother being unusually quiet, which stirred her unease. As Denise peered out the window, she recalled the unnaturally deepening darkness outside. Denise's mother recognized by looking at the skies that this was no drill.

As they raced home the smooth interstate gave way to an unmanicured gravel road. Tina's rear-wheel drive car sped true to its destination at the farm, leaving them seconds before the tornado bore down on them.

As Denise peeked out the window, she spotted a cloud she had never seen before. The top of this cloud churned at the top, rolling like someone was twirling a rope. A dark and ominous cone formed right before her eyes. Curiosity swiftly morphed into fear. This was the very tornado she had only seen in pictures.

They ran towards the storm cellar in the basement as they arrived at the family farm.

Basements are scary places when you're a kid, and Denise lived in one of the scariest ones of them all. She recalls the basement at the farm being a location where nightmares were created... dark, musty, and a favorite location for all things evil, like spiders. It was an old storm cellar that was built to shelter a family in case of a tornado, and today, it was going to earn its keep by safeguarding her and her family.

As Denise and her mother ran into the cellar for shelter, she vividly remembers sensing her mother's energy becoming even more heightened. And then… it hit.

"As the tornado approached, I remember everything shaking for about a minute. I heard what sounded like a train. I pictured the tornado going through trees," she recalls, "then… nothing".

The aftermath of a tornado is a curious time, much like a train passing overhead and then going silent immediately afterward. "After the shaking stopped, I didn't know if our home was still there."

Eventually, Denise and her mother made their way out of the cellar.

As she looked out, she recalled wondering where the nearby trailer was. Structures that aren't affixed are usually the most susceptible to being tossed in the air. When a twister hits, these are the most dangerous places to be. Denise was unaware of it then, but this locomotive of a tornado had done more than pick up their nearby trailer.

In reality, Denise and her mother had just won the twister lottery.

The tornado destroyed the neighbor's house, hopped over their home, and then swallowed up the house on the other side of theirs. The cyclone picked up the neighbor's nearby barn and deposited it a half-mile away, standing upright where it landed.

The mighty F-4 tornado exacted a heavy toll on Churubusco, damaging about half the buildings and homes while uprooting almost every tree in the friendly town. Somehow, it failed to claim a single life during its rampage. The people of Churubusco were spared.

Tornados are a lot like insurrections. Their energy and destructive aftermath are unknown until afterward.

Growing up in Columbus, Indiana, surely former Vice-President Mike Pence knew the destruction that could occur when tornados unleash their fury. Yet, on January 6, 2021, his brush with death wasn't caused by Mother Nature's rampaging winds. It was caused by humans carrying guns, knives, and a guillotine with his name on it.

Like a deadly twister, there were plenty of signs that trouble was brewing before the event. Three days before the insurrection, former President Trump approved activating the National Guard. However, this support was used primarily as traffic support for the day's events. Officials quelled the use of more force due to earlier widespread criticism of helicopters and strong National Guard presence against crowds who turned out for the George Floyd protests in a previous demonstration in Washington D.C.[12]

Many people who survive storms don't live through it for any reason other than luck, and sometimes mere seconds separates survival from death. How close was Mike Pence on January 6th to being caught in the storm we know as the Insurrection? Let's look at the timeline for Mike Pence's brush with disaster as it unfolded.

1:00 pm: As Trump's "Stop the Steal" rally ends, around 5,000 protestors march to the U.S. Capitol Building. The protest quickly turns into a destructive riot as Trump supporters break through three barricades on the Northwest side and clash with DC Police.

1:03 pm-1:30 pm: House Speaker Nancy Pelosi bangs the gavel to a joint session of Congress to count the electoral votes. Senator Paul Gosar, joined by Senator Ted Cruz, rose to question the electoral results of his state of Arizona. Senate Majority Leader Mitch McConnel solemnly warns Congress about overruling the will of the voters, saying it would "damage our Republic Forever." They are unaware that the mob has broken through the final police barricades and now have unfiltered access to the Capitol.

Shortly after 2 p.m, the first rioters climbed into the U.S. Capitol while a tsunami of other rioters followed, beating up Capitol police who stood in their way.

2:13 pm: Seconds can be the difference between life and death for those caught in a tornado, and on January 6th, seconds may have

[12] Clevenger, Andrew. "DC Guard Chief Details Pentagon Delays during Jan. 6 Riot at Capitol." Roll Call, March 3, 2021. https://rollcall.com/2021/03/03/d-c-guard-chief-details-pentagon-delays-during-jan-6-riot-at-capitol/.

spared Mike Pence's life. The Secret Service felt they could wait no longer, and they hurriedly escorted him, his wife, and his daughter from the Senate Chamber to a nearby office.

2:14 pm: Officer Eugene Goodman diverts the mob away from the Senate Chambers, allowing senators and Mike Pence to scramble and escape.

Mike Pence hunkered down in a loading dock with his family and security aides in an underground parking garage[13] while the insurrection raged inside and outside the Capitol.

Let's step back. The Vice President of the United States, one of the most powerful people in the free world, was *in an underground parking garage* while an angry mob above him tore its path of destruction from the White House Lawn and breached into the Capitol.

The Secret Service has stated that the former Vice-President was always secure during the insurrection. Yet, if the rioters had arrived seconds earlier, they would have seen the Vice President as he sought safety.

So let's get back to that question... how the %$&! could this have happened?

Like you, I watched in horror as the events on January 6th unfolded. Unfortunately, I was not surprised when they occurred.

Earlier, I introduced you to the field of Revolution Science. Another one of my mentors, Ted Gurr, author of "Why Men Rebel," offers what I feel was the best explanation for that day.

---

[13] Cole, Brendan. "Mike Pence Hid in 'Loading Dock' in Parking Garage during January 6 Riot." Newsweek, November 9, 2021. https://www.newsweek.com/mike-pence-january-6-riot-loading-dock-underground-parking-garage-1647353.

Gurr theorized that almost all uprisings follow a "frustration-aggression" pattern. In short, the more incredible the frustration from a group of citizens, the greater the aggression.

What makes Revolution Analysts and me *uber* nervous is how quickly we seem to be migrating into one of these patterns. Civil wars and revolutions sometimes take decades before they come to fruition. In the last several years, though, we've catapulted from civil political disagreements to destructive insurrections.

Accelerants speed up the energy needed to start the actual uprising. Sometimes, the accelerant is an event, like the fall of the Berlin Wall prior to the collapse of the USSR, and other times, it's the return of a leader, like Ayatollah Khomeini, before the Iranian Revolution of 1979.

Yet today's modern accelerants include both social media and biased news and have the ability to incite dangerous and deadly behavior from some people, as evidenced on January 6th, 2021.

Tim Kendall, a former executive at Pinterest and Facebook, gave a landmark testimony at the House Committee on Energy and Commerce on September 4th, 2020. He said, "I wanted to improve the world we all lived in. Instead, the social media services that I and others have built have torn people apart with alarming speed and intensity."

That last sentence, "with alarming speed and intensity," frightens me the most.

Tristan Harris, a former design ethicist at Google, has sounded the alarm at how quickly the messages on social media can radicalize some Americans. Tristan explains, "If you want to control the population of a country, there has never been a tool as effective as Facebook."

We can no longer say the plans by domestic terrorists to kidnap the Michigan Governor in 2020 or the US Insurrection in 2021 are isolated events.

Before we move forward, though, just a reminder, we are still a democracy of the people. Insurrectionists, extremists, and media sources who profit by keeping us divided don't get to control the future of our country – we do—you and me.

Let's start this evolution back into normalcy by examining our thoughts about the current political climate in the United States.

Most people nod in agreement or reaffirm a comment on social media when someone states, "We've never been more polarized." I get it. It just seems easier to agree with their statement than to challenge their belief.

How about when someone states that those without college are more likely to be extremists? I've heard this one quite frequently.

Yet, are those statements actually true? (For the record, this study found that 60% of the individuals who were prosecuted for the insurrection had at least some college - including 37% who had college degrees.[14])

A great article in The Atlantic offered some insight: "There is no doubt that polarization influences democratic ideals and principles. It is also true that research shows conclusively that we perceive ourselves to be more polarized than what we are".

We have to ask ourselves, if we're not as divided as we think, then why do both left-leaning and right-leaning media sources state we are? You'll see in future chapters the real reason (hint: it's moola - gotta get those clicks!) and what we can do to fight back against this toxicity.

Think about it. Political pundits, politicians, and journalists constantly tell us, "We're a hopelessly divided and polarized nation."

---

[14] Nietzel, 2023

If we're relentlessly pounded with that same rhetoric every day. Eventually, many will believe it. Your brain goes into what I call 'Tesla Self-Driving Mode,' and you mindlessly answer the question without reviewing your beliefs.

I think most agree that a democracy should have healthy disagreement. However, today's problems are more profound than a few healthy debates. The difference today is our largest online media and cable news sources are being paid to divide us, and that factor is significantly driving Americans further apart.

This chapter's bite-size learning is about an NLP (Neuro-linguistic Programming) hack called *reframing*. Reframing teaches people to re-route damaging limiting beliefs and replace them with more accurate (and positive) thoughts.

When we trigger a transformation by replacing inaccurate beliefs with positive affirmations, something intriguing happens: hope appears. In the book "Beyond Conflict," Timothy Phillips and his contributors show just how this change takes place in a struggling nation when we emphasize our shared values rather than our divisions[15].

If you've finished the training, let's return to the question I posed earlier in the book...could a Civil War, Revolution, or long-term uprising occur in the United States?

Unfortunately, scientific findings indicate that numerous elements resembling those observed in past uprisings are converging in the United States, raising the potential for such a scenario to become a reality.

---

15 Phillips, Timothy, Mary Albon, Ina Breuer, David Taffel, Václav Havel, David Ervine, and Leonel Gómez. Beyond Conflict: The Project On Justice In Times of Transition: 20 Years Of Putting Experience To Work For Peace. Cambridge, MA: Project on Justice in Times of Transition, 2013.

In the upcoming chapter, we'll delve deeper into the realm of Revolution Science and explore the telltale signs that should serve as a cautionary signal for both citizens and our government.

Chapter 2

Can Technology Really Predict a Civil War? There's an App for That

You just read about a blind spot we all share called limiting beliefs. They're produced by inherent biases, family, education, experiences, and outside sources you believe to be true.

The reason we call it a blind spot is many times, these limiting beliefs sit in your unconscious.

At best, these limiting beliefs fight to save you the stress and discomfort of dealing with something difficult, like not leaving a job you hate because you believe you're not good enough for what you really want to do.

However, at their worst, these limiting beliefs produce artificial truth bombs inside us, negatively influencing how we see others. We saw these beliefs in plain sight during the insurrection when thousands of protestors converged upon the Capitol, believing an election had been stolen.

Let's read about a germ-fighting scientist named Ignaz Semmelweis and the lesson he provides for us to deal with limiting beliefs. You may not have heard of him, but you have him to thank for saving countless lives and a little-known reflex we all make when judging others.

Semmelweis was a Hungarian physician and scientist in the 19th century. He worked at two maternity clinics: one that primarily utilized medical students to deliver babies and another that utilized midwives.

However, Ingza had a problem: the first clinic that utilized medical students to deliver babies had a much higher mortality rate than the second clinic that primarily utilized midwives. In fact, this difference was so great that women would sometimes resort to giving birth in the streets rather than being admitted to the first clinic. Yes, it was that bad.

Ingza was puzzled and perplexed: How could the first clinic experience such a proportionally higher mortality rate when both hospitals were doing the same thing?

This mystery plagued him until one important event: the death of his good friend, Jakob Kolletschka.

In 1847, Ingza's friend Jakob Kolletschka, also a physician, was performing a routing autopsy alongside a student when he was accidentally poked by the student's scalpel being used to perform the autopsy.

Kolletschka became ill and soon died following this examination.

Upon scrutinizing his friend's final days of good health, Ingza came to the realization that his friend had succumbed to the same illness that had claimed the lives of numerous maternity patients due to a bacterial infection. The perplexing question that arose was: How?

Of particular importance were the pre-surgery routines between students and midwives. Ingza realized that the students did little to wash their hands in between working on autopsies and working on delivering babies in the maternity section of the clinic.

To test his hypothesis, Ingza instituted a policy of using a solution of chlorinated lime for washing hands in between autopsy work and the examination of patients. Alas! The results were astonishing after the hospital adopted this policy. The mortality rate in the first clinic declined almost immediately from 18.3% to under 2.5% within two months.

Yet this story takes a dark turn for our germ-fighting hero after his breakthrough discovery.

Semmelweis and his students began a campaign to educate the medical community on their breakthrough, yet its integration of this practice was slow. Some physicians even felt offended at his findings, believing there was little correlation between the practice and lower mortality rates.

Semmelweis was outraged! He turned on the medical community, even writing an open letter to prominent obstetricians calling them "irresponsible murderers." Remember, back then, an open letter held as much weight as calling out your opponent on Twitter. Both are ill-advised.

This stress was not easy on Semmelweis. His mental and physical health deteriorated rapidly following the shunning of his findings, and in the summer of 1865, he was referred to a mental institution on advice from his physician.

Semmelweis was severely beaten by several guards when he attempted an escape while held in the institution. The beatings caused a severe infection. He died in August of 1865 from a gangrenous wound due to an infection on his right hand.[16]

---

[16] "Ignaz Semmelweis," Wikipedia, August 21, 2023, https://en.wikipedia.org/wiki/Ignaz_Semmelweis#Breakdown_and_death.

Our poor hero! Yet there's a silver lining to this story because Semmelweis lives on in posthumous glory.

Years later, rock stars of the scientific world like Louis Pasteur and other dignitaries gave widespread credit to his discovery in germ theory. Yet this credit certainly did not come right away. Today, it sounds unreal that physicians wouldn't take the time to wash their hands to prevent infection, yet that's exactly what occurred.

How long do you think it took the medical community to accept the practice of handwashing as a standard medical practice after his discovery?

Take the very brief online quiz titled "Wash Your Hands! Survey[17]" to discover the answer. You'll see the link for the quiz in the footnotes below.

If you took the quiz, the answer to this question may have surprised you. Yet besides being credited for his findings in germ theory, our hero Semmelweis is also known for something we are also guilty of, called... you guessed it... the 'Semmelweis Reflex.' The Semmelweis Reflex is the tendency to reject new knowledge that conflicts with norms and traditions.

And here is where the link between Semmelweis and modern politics collide.

There is plenty of statistical data about why uprisings and civil wars occur. This data is readily available to our world leaders as a barometer to understand how close their country is to sliding into a civil war or a prolonged uprising. Yet, for the most part... this data is largely ignored.

It should not be. I've read numerous social media posts, some even from politicians, that casually argue a civil war or revolution is the

---

[17] https://www.surveymonkey.com/r/8ZQHDYZ

answer to their misguided quest for improving our country. It should be the last thing we should ever desire for ourselves and future generations.

No expression regarding an internal revolt has been more accurate than the words of Mao Tse Tung, who once said, "A revolution is not a dinner party."

Civil wars are costly, destructive, and deadly. There were 655,000 deaths during the American Civil War (by far the bloodiest conflict in our history). An estimated 6,800 Americans were killed in the Revolutionary War (tens of thousands more died of disease, and still more were wounded in action or taken prisoner). Nine of the fifty-six Declaration of Independence signers fought and died in the American Revolution[18].

In the most severe uprisings, like the Taiping Revolution in China from 1850 to 1864, 30 million deaths occurred.

For those who think it could never occur here, I get it; our last civil war was over 170 years ago. Yet, the signs of some future type of disturbance in the United States are becoming overwhelming. That drumbeat of civil war or some other type of uprising in the United States is only getting louder and louder and louder, much of it due to misguided politicians simply seeking clicks on social media.

So, let's answer that earlier question: If we are getting closer to a civil war, is there just an app that our nation's leaders can download from Google and use it to predict how close we are to an uprising?

---

[18] "American Revolution Facts." American Battlefield Trust, August 24, 2021. http://battlefields.org/learn/articles/american-revolution-faqs#:~:text=Throughout%20the%20course%20of%20the%20war%2C%20an%20estimated%206%2C800%20Americans,died%20while%20prisoners%20of%20war).

Well… sort of. It may disappoint you to find out that there's no app you can download that tells you where the next uprisings will occur in the world. Yet there are surprisingly stable amounts of variables linked to political instability.

For example, Erica Chenoweth and Maria J. Stephan, authors and political scientists, tracked uprisings from 1900 to 2006. What they discovered is that it takes around "3.5% of the population actively participating in the protests to ensure serious political change.[19]"

It may also surprise you that companies and organizations can accurately predict where civil unrest is most likely.

How do they do it?

These organizations capture a plethora of economic, political, and environmental data points, and then put them into a magic algorithm that weighs a country's likelihood of increased civil unrest. These 'country risk assessments' are used for both business and other social reasons.

The intelligence they offer helps an organization anticipate strategic threats in countries where they have business. It provides a barometer to proactively manage trends before they emerge.

Crazy, right?

Some of you may think these 'country risk assessments' are just tools the misinformation armies are using to drum up conflict, but there's an important reason why these predictions are accurate.

[19] David Robson, "The '3.5% Rule': How a Small Minority Can Change the World," BBC Future, March 3, 2023, https://www.bbc.com/future/article/20190513-it-only-takes-35-of-people-to-change-the-world.

Companies like Verisk Maplecroft have captured data from centuries of uprisings to help their clients understand the chances for disruption in a country. What makes their reporting even more amazing is how deeply they understand the consequences of coups and other conflicts.

One such recent example is Verisk Maplecroft's coverage of the coup in Myanmar, a nation of 54 million people in Southeast Asia.[20] The country is known for its lucrative energy, mining, and infrastructure.

Fast forward to February 1, 2021, when the military seized control of the government following a general election in which Myanmar's National League for Democracy party had won by a landslide.

Following this landslide, a military leader, General Hlaing, spread misinformation about widespread election fraud. This is a common tactic used by dictators and other authoritarian leaders. The election fraud claim was all he needed, and soon after, he seized power "on the side of the people."

The military jailed Myanmar's democratically elected leader, Aung San Suu Kyi. The citizens of Myanmar were outraged and took to the streets to protest the military coup and their loss of individual rights.

These protests have been ruthlessly suppressed by the ruling military. In their wake, an estimated 4,000 activists have been killed.[21]

Unfortunately, things have gotten worse for the citizens of Myanmar since the military coup.

---

20 Jess Middleton, "The Trendline - Global Political Risk at Highest Level in Five Years," Verisk Maplecroft, February 2, 2023, https://www.maplecroft.com/insights/analysis/risk-signals-global-political-risk-at-highest-level-in-five-years/.

21 "Assistance Association for Political Prisoners." Assistance Association for Political Prisoners. Accessed August 23, 2023. https://aappb.org/.

Fast forward to 2023: the country is grappling with a 3rd wave of COVID-19, and healthcare workers who support protestors have been jailed en masse, with at least 30 killed.[22]

There's something extra to this story that I believe is important to note.

The uprising and takeover of the country by the military in Myanmar following what they proclaim was widespread election fraud is almost an exact playbook of what bad actors in the 'stop the steal' conspiracy camp in the United States are following.

You may think that the January 6th hearings proved we are over that crisis, yet the election deniers have had two years to re-organize. Later in the book, we'll discuss the two very viable (and legal) paths for disrupting our 2024 Presidential race and beyond.

Let's dig a little deeper into the study of uprisings and see what other experts say. The experts I write about are not columnists or weekend authors. They are people and organizations that thoroughly study uprisings and their causes.

Many data points companies use to predict uprisings were created by early pioneers who studied civil wars and revolutions.

One early pioneer was Ted Robert Gurr. A scientist and social psychologist at heart, Gurr first became interested in studying signs of civil wars and other uprisings in the 1980s. In his book, "*Why Men Rebel,* Gurr theorized that political violence could be explained by social psychology and other socioeconomic data.[23]

---

[22] Green, Lindsay. "'Our Health Workers Are Working in Fear': After Myanmar's Military Coup, One Year of Targeted Violence against Health Care." PHR, January 28, 2022. https://phr.org/our-work/resources/one-year-anniversary-of-the-myanmar-coup-detat/.

[23] Ted Robert Gurr, essay, in *Why Men Rebel* (London: Routledge, Taylor & Francis Group, 2016), 24-25.

In 1994-1995, he helped create the Political Instability Task Force for the Clinton Administration. This data has been critical in several ways. For example, he offered input at the 2004 Stockholm International Forum on the Prevention of Genocide and collaborated with others to assess countries at risk for political unrest, which I term "Revolution Science."

Chapter 3

Seductive Dictators and An Early Warning System for Uprisings

Would it surprise you that statistics in 2023 show democracy is backsliding throughout the world? In fact, according to Luhrmann and Lindberg, "the third wave of autocratization" is accelerating and deepening." For the first time since 2001, democracies are no longer the majority.

The Carnegie Endowment for International Peace reports that the democratic countries of India, El Salvador, Mexico, Israel, and Tunisia have all seen democratic guard rails, such as fair and free elections, erode and in steady decline.[24]

Revolution Science reveals an important pattern observed in countries transitioning away from democracy to alternate forms of government, and this trend should serve as a warning to the United States: the emergence of civil wars.

Luminous author Barbara F. Walters points out, "Since 1946, right after World War II ended, the number of democracies in the world

[24] Carothers, 2023

had surged - but so had the number of civil wars. They seemed to be rising in tandem.[25]"

But why does this occur?

First, new leaders transitioning into democracy just can't walk into a Barnes and Noble and purchase the book "Democracy for Dummies." The transition from authoritarian-style leadership to democracy is messy at best.

Imagine how your life would be upended under a regime change. Suddenly, your family faces a spike in food and energy prices, and your children now attend a different school with a vastly different curriculum.

Furthermore, your nation might encounter a power vacuum, accompanied by the diminishing influence of many powerful citizens who will regroup and fight to regain their lost power and prestige. Sometimes, a country's migration into democracy does not survive this turbulent change.

Earlier, we listed some of the countries experiencing a democratic backslide. There's one more country we need to add to this watchlist of failing democracies: the United States.

What are some of the early warning indicators of unrest that we're currently witnessing in the United States? We've listed some of them in this chapter. Please note these are only a few of the data points the science uses to track a nation's instability.

---

[25] Walter, 2023,24

Uprising Early Warning Indicator #1: The Seductive Dictator Trap

In the United States, we're accustomed to hearing about major conflicts in nations other than ours. These revolutions and uprisings, which often take decades to develop, typically reveal clues before they occur.

We are witnessing some of these clues in our country in real-time. For example, most people feel we've never been more divided in our nation, and this feeling is characteristic of some type of imminent trouble ahead.

Yet many times, a country's leadership fails to take action during this time, or simply ignores the signs, before the actual uprising.

Ted Gurr offers insight into this missed opportunity a country's leader has before a rebellion: "Ignorance is almost always among its causes: sometimes ignorance of consequences by those who resort to it, but more often by ignorance by those who create and maintain the social conditions that inspire it.[26]"

As we read earlier, a significant event, like the fall of the Berlin Wall, or the return of a leader who promises to rebuild the country to its former place as a world power, are all it takes to plunge a country into chaos.

The first early warning sign has been witnessed throughout history: the rise of the seductive leader.

It would be challenging to find individuals today who regard figures like Hitler, Mussolini, and other destroyers of humanity as leaders

[26] Gurr,24

who truly benefited their nations. Yet that's exactly what their citizens believed as they rose to power.

At times, these leaders moved the country from one form of government to another all in the name of 'progress'.

In the democracy death spiral, democratic ideals start to yield to what Law Professor Ozan Varol describes as "stealth authoritarianism." The country, once brimming with hope and the aspiration of enhanced freedoms, gradually drifts away from democratic principles and reverts to anti-democratic practices.

The movement only lacks one resounding voice, promising the citizens better wages, more effective governance, and a return to a time when the nation held greater global influence.

Whether by force, like the 2020 military takeover in Myanmar, or voted into office via free elections, the shift from democracy to autocratic leadership always has an expert con man ready to sell the story that reversing course back to the glory days is what the country needs.

Sometimes, these leaders represent a true voice of change for the people, and sometimes the appointed leader pushes for their own ideological ways while destroying the culture and people they've campaigned to improve.

You just read earlier how difficult it is to transition from an autocracy to a democratic nation. Many countries have tried and succeeded, yet many collapsed back into the same rigid political structure they had before.

Renew Democracy, a non-partisan organization aimed at defending democracy, states that this can occur for many reasons. Democracies fall when elites feel democracy "no longer works for them," and economies falter, pushing voters to seek extreme options in a candidate.[27] This leader often provides just what its citizens want to hear: a return to "the good old days."

But these leaders share another common trait: the role of passionate rescuer and the misguided belief that they are 'saving' the country from outright disaster. The dictator becomes larger than life and begins to believe the illusory lie of what the pundits around him/her are telling him. They have become victims of what Brian Klaas calls "The Dictator Trap."

Let's do a little neuro-linguistic experiment and learn why these dictators often rise to power.

In this experiment, we'll compare the common attributes people state they want in a boss and compare them with attributes we claim we want when choosing a President.

In the space below or on your favorite note-taking phone app, write down the top 3 attributes your favorite manager has had. You know, the boss everyone thought was great? Don't think about it too long; just write what comes to mind. You'll read what others have said in an upcoming paragraph.

____

____

____

[27] "From Democracy to Dictatorship." RDI, August 21, 2023. https://rdi.org/articles/from-democracy-to-dictatorship/.

*The answers are charisma, assertiveness, and competence. Are you surprised?

Ok great. Now, guess which are the *actual* reasons many people get hired into leadership positions? (Please see the footnote below after answering*)

Do you see the differences? So why do we get choosing competent leaders so *wrong*?

Let me introduce you to Organizational Psychologist Tomas Chamorro-Premuzic. Tomas studies human behavior in the workplace and, more specifically, why some people become leaders.

According to Tomas, "There is a pathological mismatch between the qualities that seduce us in a leader and those that are needed to be a leader.[28]"

He goes on to state, "empathy, helping people feel like they matter, and emotional intelligence" are desired attributes of a leader. Yet, think about how many managers you've worked for who have these attributes.

And we may have ourselves to blame for this.

Tomas says that when it comes to choosing a leader, "we go for people who are confident rather than competent. We tend to go for people who are charismatic instead of being humble." And sometimes, we even choose people who are narcissistic rather than honest.

Sometimes, this leader's seduction is irresistible to our primitive ego.

---

[28] Chamorro-Premuzic, Tomas. "Why Do So Many Incompetent Men Become Leaders?" Harvard Business Review, February 27, 2023. https://hbr.org/2013/08/why-do-so-many-incompetent-men.

Does this sound like how we choose a President at times?

Perhaps there is no greater example of this seduction trap than Russia's Vladimir Putin, the architect of Russia's democratic death spiral. Putin's reckless disregard for consequences and blinding allegiance to his nationalistic ideology puts his country's citizens in harm's way for possible darker days ahead.

You previously learned that civil wars and unrest are highly likely when a country transitions quickly from autocracy to democracy. Yet Putin's honeymoon with democracy is over. As Professor Karen Dawisha, a former Professor of Political Science at Miami University, writes, "Instead of seeing Russia as a democracy in a process that's failing, we're seeing it as an authoritarian system that's succeeding."

Let's review how Putin and Russia got to this place in history.

Vladimir Putin has enjoyed a successful career as an elected official, winning two elections and serving as president from 2000-2008, then remaining in the position after his second election in 2012.

Freedoms in Russia have plummeted since his second rule began in 2012. He crushed independent TV, pushed out his political challengers, and locked up thousands of anti-war protestors. This backsliding has also produced widespread corruption, and a crackdown on the free press.[29] While it's difficult to find accurate statistics from Russia, General Mark Milley estimates that over 200,000 Russian and Ukrainian soldiers have been killed in the conflict.[30]

---

[29] Judah, Ben. "How Putin Plunged Russia toward Totalitarianism." Slate Magazine, March 10, 2022. https://slate.com/news-and-politics/2022/03/putin-russia-totalitarianism-soviet-style-oppression.html.

[30] "Ukraine War: US Estimates 200,000 Military Casualties on All Sides." BBC News, November 10, 2022. https://www.bbc.com/news/world-europe-63580372.

For these reasons, it is remarkable that this did not produce Russia's first Civil War since the 1917 Bolshevik Rebellion. For the most part, Russia has defied an uprising, and democracy has survived. Until now.

The Russian disinformation machine, like ours, has, for a time, been able to keep a large part of the Russian people supporting the war. Yet my prediction is that this popularity is unstable at best.

History shows this popularity may eventually give way to widespread condemnation of the war as the Russian people mourn over their sons and daughters returning from the war in body bags, and economic disparity continues. With rising casualties, Russian citizens may turn against Putin's war sooner rather than later. As of July 31st, 2023, 9,369 civilians have been killed, and over 16,646 have been injured in this conflict.[31]

Like most dictators, Putin employs a strategy of fear to keep control of Russia. Indeed, he does not take criticism well. Publicly speaking out against Putin has been risky, and a long line of Putin's public enemy's seemingly had terrible luck, including Yevgeny Prigozhin, a Putin critic who was killed after his private plane "accidentally" fell out of the sky in August 2023.

Russian journalist Yuri Shchekochikhin and Russian Defector Alexander Litvinenko, both critical of Putin's regime, mysteriously died from poisoning. Other Putin detractors, like Russian Journalist Anna Politkovskaya and politician Sergei Yushenkov, were assassinated.

One of his most vocal opponents, Alexei Navalny, was given a highly toxic nerve agent that should have killed him. He now resides in a

[31] "Ukraine: Civilian Casualty Update 31 July 2023." OHCHR, July 31, 2023. https://www.ohchr.org/en/news/2023/07/ukraine-civilian-casualty-update-31-july-2023#:~:text=Total%20civilian%20casualties,9%2C369%20killed%20and%2016%2C646%20injured.

Moscow jail with little luck of ever being released without a regime change.

None of these deaths are directly tied to Putin, yet dictators punish those who challenge them, and Putin's involvement in their demise seems likely, according to Sky News.[32]

The former KGB Officer has now tilted Russian democracy to the brink of collapse with broken promises of free elections, mass incarcerations of his people, and worldwide condemnation for the carnage in Ukraine he's responsible for.

Yet this fall of democracy doesn't just affect Russia and Ukraine. His actions reverberate into the entire world. The ending for Putin seems bleak based upon his reckless war with Ukraine and how history has judged this type of leader in the past.

His downfall may move Russia into dangerous territory as forces for democracy and forces for autocracy clash over ideals. The world awaits, yet one thing is certain: with nuclear weapons and humanity at stake, an unstable Russia is a dangerous Russia.

As you've learned in Revolution Science, often, one data point doesn't necessarily trigger an uprising, and as we've learned with Vladimir Putin, the actions of a reckless leader sometimes aren't enough to trigger a regime change.

Yet it appears Putin's mighty grip on power and public opinion is waning.

Putin's vulnerability was unmasked on June 24, 2023, as Yevgeny Prigozhin, once a friend of Vladimir Putin, came within 250 miles

---

32 "The Putin Critics Who Have Been Assassinated." Sky News. Accessed August 23, 2023. https://news.sky.com/story/the-putin-critics-who-have-been-assassinated-10369350.

of having his mercenaries enter Moscow in protest to the Russian military attacking one of his camps.[33]

Wager Group leader Yevgeny Prigozhin claimed that the regular Russian army had launched a missile strike on the Wagner mercenaries' rear camps on June 23, 2023. Prigozhin (a former friend of Putin's) was galvanized into action, sending 25,000 mercenaries "to restore justice" by seizing Russian military facilities and shooting down Russian helicopters. As the mercenaries marched toward Moscow, it became clear that they were planning a coup. In an emergency address on June 24th, Putin said that Russia is "fighting for survival" and there are attempts to "organize a rebellion" in the country. The rebellion was quelled when neighboring Belarus brokered a deal between the two sides.[34]

Frequently, other events unrelated to the leader's hubris provide the kindling to spark an uprising… which leads us to the 2nd Uprising Early Warning Indicator and how it's related to the growing American middle-class rage.

Uprising Early Warning Indicator #2:

The Law of Rising Expectations and the Decline of the Middle Class

"When rich speculators prosper
While farmers lose their land
When government officials spend money
On weapons instead of cure

---

[33] TYSHCHENKO, KATERYNA. "Wagner Group Now Just 400 Km Away from Moscow." Ukrainska Pravda, June 24, 2023. https://www.pravda.com.ua/eng/news/2023/06/24/7408365/.

[34] Belton, Catherine. "Putin Appeared Paralyzed and Unable to Act in First Hours of Rebellion." The Washington Post, July 26, 2023. https://www.washingtonpost.com/world/2023/07/25/putin-prigozhin-rebellion-kremlin-disarray/.

When the upper class is extravagant and irresponsible
While the poor have nowhere to turn –
All this is robbery and chaos."

If you had to guess, who do you think wrote the protest statement? I would give you a thumbs-up emoji if you thought of Karl Marx, Thomas Jefferson, or even Ram Dass, who has written extensively about workers' rights.

Yet this statement was written in the Tao Te Ching, a Chinese class text, over 2,500 years ago. The correlation between uprisings and disgruntled workers is one of the most common and powerful reasons for uprisings, and as you can see from the poem above, has been noted throughout history.

But what psychological reasons exist for this long-standing battle between the "haves" and the "have-nots" so prevalent in society?

Humans inherently like to know where we stand compared to others. Psychologists call this 'social comparison,' which is a natural way to evaluate how we're doing compared to others.

On the surface, this may seem wrong to some of you. I know what you're saying: "I don't care if my best friend bought that new iPhone or just took that vacation to Bali and stayed in a hut overlooking the ocean. I want the best for them!" You consciously may want the best for your friends and family, but in reality, there's no way to turn this comparison switch off. Unfortunately, that's just not how our neurons work.

Psychologists Kedia, Mussweiler, and Linden write in their study that "what seems to characterize people's subjective well-being is not only how much they own in absolute terms, but also how they own in *comparison with others.*[35]" So, you're trying to keep up with the

[35] Kedia, Gayannée, Thomas Mussweiler, and David E J Linden. "Brain Mechanisms of Social Comparison and Their Influence on the Reward

Joneses? Blame it on biology (and that generous credit line availability you have with Citibank).

Our neurons are continually seeking massive amounts of data, some for self-improvement purposes and some to gauge how well you're doing in comparison to others.

Ted Gurr, a pioneer in the field of conflict and instability, wrote extensively about the dark side of comparative cognitive thinking.[36] Alongside this social comparison is what Gurr called *progressive deprivation*, in which a person feels their "status" in a country has been slighted due to reasons beyond their control. Daniel Lerner, Ph.D. Internal Communication at MIT called this 'the revolution of rising expectations."

When a class of people who once experienced greater social status in their life feels this status threatened, trouble is brewing.

One of the things you'll continually see when you review why countries have gone through an uprising is the disparity of wealth distributed amongst its citizens. Now, this doesn't affect all countries. In fact, studies show that if a person has never experienced wealth or the opportunity to climb the wealth ladder, this becomes a non-factor.[37]

It is also rare to see uprisings in countries with a strong middle class. According to a study by the Organization for Economic Co-Operation and Development (OECD), uprisings are almost non-existent.

Happy Middle Class = Happy Country.

System." Neuroreport, November 12, 2014. https://www.ncbi.nlm.nih.gov/pmc/articles/PMC4222713/.

[36] "Ted Robert Gurr." AAPSS, May 4, 2023. https://www.aapss.org/fellow/ted-robert-gurr/.

[37] Gurr, 24.

According to the OECD, societies with a strong middle class "have lower crime rates, they enjoy higher levels of trust and life satisfaction. Yet the one factor most political leaders should keep in mind is this: a strong middle class also is a sign of political stability.[38]"

Recently, though, keeping the middle class economically viable has gone terribly wrong in the United States and other democratic countries. Statista Research Service states, "The CEO-to-worker" compensation ratio has exploded, causing the gap between rich and poor to grow… with the largest gap since right before the Great Depression."

This wealth gap increased even more during the COVID-19 crisis of 2020-2022. Think about how this disparity between the 'haves' and 'have nots' played out in your family. If you owned a $400,000 home in 2020, you saw its value climb approximately 39% in two years, giving you $160,000 in equity. A climbing stock market helped your pocketbook grow even further.

Yet, if you were a renter during this same time, you saw the average rent climb 23%-39% and your savings account plunge.[39] So, while your wealthier parents were enjoying record wealth gains, you fell even further behind on the economic ladder.

Share of adults in U.S. middle class has decreased considerably since 1971

% of adults in each income tier

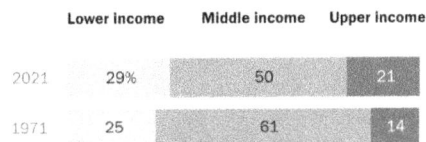

	Lower income	Middle income	Upper income
2021	29%	50	21
1971	25	61	14

[38] OECD (2019), Under Pressure: The Squeezed Middle Class, OECD Publishing, Paris https://doi.org/10.1787/689afed1-en

[39] Alcantara, Chris Alcantara, Abha Bhattarai, and Andrew Van Dam. "Rents Are Rising Everywhere. See How Much Prices Are Up in Your Area." The Washington Post, April 21, 2022. https://www.washingtonpost.com/business/interactive/2022/rising-rent-prices/.

Do you think this has caused some generational angst? Absolutely.

Additionally, disparity amongst minorities continues to grow even more.

That feeling of wealth disparity has got to go somewhere, and many times, it shows its ugly head in a pervasive way: a rise in rage and nationalism amongst those in the lower wealth brackets.

However, there are additional clues besides economic disparity that are generating concerns about some type of uprising in the United States.

One surprising component has also occurred alongside civil wars and other uprisings throughout history and can shake governments to their core. Unfortunately, we should know this element very well, so let's learn about Uprising Early Indicator #3.

Uprising Early Warning Indicator #3: Global Pandemics

We just learned how faltering economic conditions, especially in the middle class, are one of the strongest conduits for uprisings. Another unique factor sometimes also appears alongside an uprising: a global pandemic.

Let's look at the Russian Revolution of 1917. As World War I drew close, the Spanish Flu spread its dangerous contagion via convenient travel partners returning home from the war on packed ships.[40]

---

[40] "History of 1918 Flu Pandemic." Centers for Disease Control and Prevention, March 21, 2018. https://www.cdc.gov/flu/pandemic-resources/1918-commemoration/1918-pandemic-history.htm.

The Spanish Flu alone did not signal the end of the Romanov dynasty and the beginning of the Russian Revolution in Russia. Still, it helped put a nail in the Romanov coffin and influenced this revolution.

Here's why: pandemics usually produce massive economic turbulence, substantial loss of life, and erode a country's ability to sustain and grow. To give you some perspective, the Black Death from 1331 – 1353 caused an estimated 75,000,000 deaths, *half of Europe's population* and an estimated 22% globally.

Norman Cohn observes in his study of violence in medieval Europe, "Again and again one finds that a particular outbreak of revolutionary chiliasm took place against a background of disaster: the plagues that precluded the First Crusade" and "the Black Death."

But pandemics sometimes seem to have at least one positive outcome: the rise of workers' standard of living. Workers pick up leverage and flex their muscles as labor shortages appear because of the pandemic.

In his article 'How the Black Death Led to the Peasants Revolt,' E.R. Zarevich confirms that England's uprising was fueled by the unrest in the aftermath of the pandemic. Trade and generating goods were disrupted, and prices of both imported and exported goods skyrocketed as workers became scarce.[41] Lords were so desperate to hire workers that the social distinction broke down. Sensing an opportunity, workers abandoned their "master" and shopped around for better wages.[42]

---

[41] Zarevich, E.R. "How the Black Death Led to the Peasants' Revolt." explorethearchive.com, July 1, 2021. https://explorethearchive.com/peasants-revolt.

[42] Courie, Leonard W. The Black Death and Peasants Revolt. New York: Wayland Publishers, 1972; Strayer, Joseph R., ed. *Dictionary of the Middle Ages*. New York: Charles Scribner's Sons. Vol. 2. pp. 257-267.

I was curious about how the COVID-19 pandemic has affected workers here in the United States and found today's worker unrest shares this common thread with their ancestors.

Like previous pandemics, worker shortages in the United States disrupted business as usual. In 2021, more than 47 million workers quit their jobs.[43] Many positions were in the service industry, while workers in other industries took this time to re-think their current positions...and lives.

Studies show this post-COVID "Great Resignation" we experienced after people began returning to work turned into the "Great Reshuffling," as most workers have found employment in other fields. Yet, this is a worker's revolt that the United States hasn't witnessed for many decades.

Social media has become the new bullhorn for uniting those disenfranchised workers in forums where they share grievances.

One of these sites dedicated to uniting disenfranchised workers is the subreddit "antiwork,"' which boasts over 2.4 million members and counting. Members do not pull punches. Posting emails about the disparity of pay amongst genders and minorities in an organization and calling out individual managers by name who have wronged them is fair game on this site dedicated to the modern-day workers' revolt.

Were you one of these workers who decided to "reshuffle"? If so, you are not alone.

Whether you feel growing equity inequality and better working conditions must be addressed or feel it's just capitalism doing its job, political leaders would be wise to listen to this middle-class angst and

[43] Ferguson, Stephanie. "Understanding America's Labor Shortage: The Most Impacted Industries." U.S. Chamber of Commerce, August 10, 2023. https://www.uschamber.com/workforce/understanding-americas-labor-shortage-the-most-impacted-industries.

act. As shown, revolts occur more commonly in those nations where large amounts of dissatisfied workers fuel the revolt, as was proven with the end of the Romanovs.

This trend of a post-pandemic worker revolt is appearing in the United States. Over the last few years, many workers have unionized or attempted to unionize, including Starbucks and Amazon employees. In fact, Unions boasted approximately 200,000 new members in 2022.[44] Big labor strikes have also occurred at John Deer, the Writer's Guild of America, and potential large strikes at UPS and the United Auto Workers were averted.[45]

As we cover these interrelated elements that produce uprisings, ask yourself: If the global and US economy turned south, could it also be another element that produces a sustained uprising? This is what scholars and companies who dive deep into data points look for when predicting a revolt.

Let's look at another warning sign that's placing stress on our democracy. This issue rapidly intensifies as biased news stations fuel culture wars, and online clickbait further divides us into opposing camps.

Uprising Early Warning Indicator #4: Collapsing Human and Democratic Rights

There is one essential psychological element related to uprisings we've seen in the news recently that should be sounding alarm bells for political and local leaders in the United States.

---

44 "Union Members Summary." *Https://www.Bls.Gov/News.Release/Union2.Nr0.Htm*. US Department of Labor, January 19, 2023. Bureau of Labor and Statistics. https://www.bls.gov/news.release/union2.nr0.htm.

45 Garver, Rob. "Major Strikes Loom in US Labor Market." VOA, July 20, 2023. https://www.voanews.com/a/major-strikes-loom-in-us-labor-market-/7189659.html.

This component is not related to a country's economic issues, pandemics, ethnic reasons, or any of the other interrelated data points common in an uprising. In a democratic society, this element speaks to the very soul of what a person will fight for. Call it *freedom, hope, liberty, democracy*, or whatever adjective you like. Studies show that citizens who enjoy these inherent freedoms, freedom to vote, freedom of religion, and individual liberties, will fight to the death to keep them.

Look no further than Ukraine's surprising defense against Russia, which began in 2022.

Ukraine became an independent country in December 1991 after the collapse of the Soviet Empire. We watch daily the atrocities Vladimir Putin calls acceptable in his thirst to regain the same Soviet empire that collapsed over 30 years ago. Yet, in their darkest hour, the Ukrainian people continue to fight against an enemy with more air power, soldiers, and military might. In the country's most remote areas, the Ukrainian people continue in their quest to retain their freedoms.

The Ukrainian people's fierce response to the Russian invasion is a perfect example of how an ordinary citizen will react when faced with losing human rights. This fight echoes in the words of Ukrainian President Zelensky, "By attacking us you see our faces. Not backs – faces."

You'll see ahead that the loss of freedoms we believe inherent could also be what sparks the revolutionary flame in the United States.

Chapter 4:

Building Better Elections and the Governor's Gambit to Replace Your Vote

We've already seen the outrage caused by the overturning of Roe v. Wade and by insurrectionists who believe their election was stolen. Another one of those foundational elements, the right to fair and free elections, is now under serious threat and could cause the largest uproar in our country since the Civil War.

There are no documented studies on what would occur in a country like ours that has had over 275 years of democracy if the masses felt *multiple foundational freedoms* were ripped away from them. Recall what authors Erica Chenoweth and Maria Stephan discovered in their research that it takes only 3.5% of citizens to force their goal of political change in a country.[46]

I fear what this tipping point looks like in the United States.

We witnessed the horrific events on January 6, 2021, as zealous citizens overtook the Capitol, causing mayhem, substantial damage, and loss of life.

---

[46] Robson, David, "The '3.5% Rule': How a Small Minority Can Change the World." BBC Future, March 3, 2023. https://www.bbc.com/future/article/20190513-it-only-takes-35-of-people-to-change-the-world.

During the January 6th hearings, there was a phrase that was supposedly associated with Abraham Lincoln in which he said, "America will never be destroyed from the outside. If we lose our freedoms, it will be because we have destroyed ourselves from within." (I did some fact-checking and discovered Lincoln never wrote those words, yet you'd have to think as he saw our nation crumbling before his eyes that he felt the essence of that message.)

I do not believe the fraction of US citizens who believe the 'stop the steal' lie is enough to cause a sustained uprising in the United States. There's enough significant united opposition to this falsehood among Republicans, Democrats, Independents, and Americans who do not endorse this theory. Any type of violence would also not be supported by local and national police.

Yet I worry about what would happen in the United States if an election was *really stolen by bad actors.*

We know there has been widespread rioting throughout the United States in the past. Yet, if an election really was stolen, I don't believe there's enough local or national law enforcement able to stop the kind of temporary destruction you'd see in the United States. Indeed, if this occurs, you may see the battleground Lincoln witnessed 160 years ago.

In my opinion, this sustained anger and motivation over the loss of freedoms may even define the bellwether event that fuels the next peaceful revolution in the United States.

And those options to legally steal a Presidential election are closer than you think.

Two viable options exist for the election conspiracy camp to succeed in their unholy quest to capture a United States Presidential election.

The first strategy is called "The Swing State Governor's Gambit." This involves replacing state electors involved in the election process with "stop the steal" loyalists who will attempt to install their candidate, even against the people's will.

According to Matt Seligman, a fellow at Yale Law School Center, "This only requires a few partisan officials who control the state government to submit an illegitimate slate of electors for their losing party's candidates.[47]"

Election deniers have seized this artificial loophole and are running with it.

In the introduction, we reported that many election-denying candidates were unsuccessful in the 2022 midterm elections. Yet even with this victory for democracy, the misinformation machine lives on and is poised to do more damage in future elections. Results were positive for democracy, but the spell of misinformation on some voters lingers on.

According to Grace Panetta of Business Insider, "Dozens of candidates who have embraced Trump's lie that the 2020 election was stolen are vying to become their state's chief election officials and governors." Election and bi-partisan officials serving on state and county boards who certified President Biden's win are quickly being replaced in Michigan and other states to carry out this fraudulent scheme.[48]

---

[47] Panetta, Grace, "How a Rogue Governor Could Steal the next Presidential Election for Trump." Business Insider, January 31, 2022. https://www.businessinsider.com/how-a-rogue-governor-could-steal-the-next-presidential-election-for-trump-2022-1?fbclid=IwAR3CCmIV2D0B-FRgqxb5dYPJAItUGZBGeZsKYy6U3gK9fDOUZJdiwSYxLVM.

[48] Elaine Cromie, "Republicans in Michigan Have Replaced Election Officials Who Certified Biden's Win," NPR, May 4, 2022, https://www.npr.org/2022/05/04/1096641003/republicans-in-michigan-have-replaced-election-officials-who-certified-bidens-wi?fbclid=IwAR0SAGoacy4F1NCYrm2GVwNVmTZkI4edMCGNxnIg1NfwPX2gT0xyp6fY0lU.

What's even more troubling is that they're not sneaking around. They are campaigning that they'll do just that – ignore the vote of the citizens in favor of whomever they choose for President.

It is now possible to imagine a rogue swing state Governor legally switching their choice from the candidate their voters chose to the opposition candidate in the 2024 Presidential election. In this nightmare scenario, we would have *two* candidates claiming the Presidency.

This is not just a few candidates who are continuing this drama; to date, more than 100 GOP primary winners back false election claims.[49]

There are other ways to render our votes useless in the future.

Enter the Independent Legislature Theory, which is another tool in the election manipulator's playbook.

The Independent Legislative Doctrine is wording in the Constitution that delegates power to administer federal elections to the states. According to Ethan Herenstein and Thomas Wolf of the Brennan Center for Justice, "It allows state legislatures the ability to solely regulate congressional elections – not governors, state judges, or even state constitutions." In short, it's an election denier's best friend.

The case that could have launched this nuclear civic weapon was Moore v. Harper, first heard by the Supreme Court in December 2022. It was an appeal by the North Carolina Legislature after the Supreme Court invalidated their badly gerrymandered congressional-

[49] Amy Gardner and Isaac Arnsdorf, "More than 100 GOP Primary Winners Back Trump's False Fraud Claims," The Washington Post, June 16, 2022, https://www.washingtonpost.com/politics/2022/06/14/more-than-100-gop-primary-winners-back-trumps-false-fraud-claims/.

district map, which put millions of North Carolina residents in congressional districts that "all but predetermined" the outcome.[50]

In the first vote in the spring of 2022, the Supreme Court justices voted 4-4 to cease the measure from moving forward, but this news is not so positive. *Four* Supreme Court justices approved of this "independent legislative" plan before Supreme Court Justice Amy Coney Barrett was sworn in.

Rick Hasen, an election law expert at the University of California, writes that if enough justices had decided to sign off on some version of this law before the 2024 election, "it could be an earthquake in American electoral power."

Most citizens do not believe in unbridled legislative power. Not Democrats, Independents, Republicans, Libertarians, or Anarchists. Yet this is what could have occurred if this doctrine passed.

You are correct if you believe that this seems like a loophole – it is. For the record, both Democratic and Republican delegations practice this form of cheating throughout the United States.

Most importantly, the Independent Legislative Doctrine would remove the people's vote in the presidential election. And there are election deniers who have already said they are willing to use this tactic if elected.

Thankfully, the Supreme Court rejected the independent state legislature theory in June 2023 by a vote of 6-3. Yet, this has not stopped states from trying to seize power.

---

[50] "North Carolina's Gerrymandered Districts Set Stage for 2024 Republican Wins," The Guardian, May 31, 2023, https://www.theguardian.com/us-news/2023/may/31/north-carolina-gerrymander-republicans-2024-us-elections.

For example, in my home state of Arizona, a 2021 bill in the Arizona House would have let lawmakers reject the results of an election and given a single elector in the legislature the power to demand that a new election be held.[51]

I hope this information helps you understand just how important you are to the health of our democracy. As you've read, there are some power-hungry people trying to game the system to invalidate your vote.

So, what are some of our defenses against this occurrence? First, consider voting for a candidate who doesn't support the "Stop the Steal" movement, regardless of which party you're involved in.

Another way legal experts have said we can prevent this forfeiture of power is one that's been needed for a long time…eliminating the Electoral College in favor of a system that puts the power of the vote back to where it belongs…in the hands of the people.

Let me offer a short and troubled history of the Electoral College voting method.

As you know, it's a "winner-take-all" type of voting method. So, if you're a lifelong Republican in a traditional blue state or a lifelong Democrat in a red state, your presidential vote is pretty much worthless. Your state hands over all electors to whoever gets the most votes.

In the 2020 Presidential election, 6,006,429 Trump votes in California and 5,259,126 Biden votes in Texas didn't count. That's over 11 million votes that had no Presidential representation. Zero, zilch.

---

[51] State of Arizona. House Bill 2596, page 35, lines 10-17 https://www.azleg.gov/legtext/55leg/2R/bills/HB2596P.pdf

The exceptions to this winner-take-all rule are Nebraska and Maine, which allow a variation of proportional voting based on the statewide vote and how their congressional districts vote. So in 2020, Nebraska gave one electoral vote to Joe Biden and 3 to Donald Trump. Way to go, Nebraska and Maine! You are leading the way in Presidential election reform.

The electoral process was *never* designed to give all citizens the right to choose the President and needs desperate updating. In fact, only white male landowners over the age of 21 had the right to vote in our earliest elections.

Deciding who gets to vote has only slowly evolved in the next 150 years: African American men were granted the right to vote in 1870, but incredibly it took another 50 years for women to be able to vote.

Let's look at the elephant (or donkey) in the room before we discuss alternatives.

You may wonder why we don't adopt a system that elects the President based on who gets the most votes.

Believe me. Many ponder this question each election year. This initiative is called "The National Popular Interstate Compact Act," which sounds like a law to negotiate car rental rates, yet is actually an agreement amongst a group of states to elect the President based upon the people's vote.

Wait, what? That would be too easy and too fair, right? Sigh… queue the sour music like when someone loses on a game show.

Indeed it is simple and fair, yet I haven't included it in my list of possible solutions below.

Regardless of how simplistic and fair this Act seems; it faces a mammoth uphill battle. Here's why: This Act can only be passed if the number of states that approve it amounts to 270 electoral votes since that's how many electoral votes are currently needed to choose the President.

Not impossible, but I imagine we discover the secret of replicating a velociraptor before this bill ever passes in those states fearful of losing power to their citizens. (By the way, if anyone out there really is working on replicating a velociraptor, can you let me know?)

So, let's take a look at some of the alternatives. You may have heard of some of these solutions that have been hiding in plain sight. These alternatives are not as radical as you think. In fact, some states, like Maine and Nebraska, have already switched to a version of proportional voting for the presidential election.

Popular alternatives include Ranked Choice Voting, Social Voting, and Proportional Popular Vote. Can you believe there are so many other better ways to run an election? I know! I didn't either until a few years ago.

Now, I've studied numerous alternatives, and I'd love to tell you there is one perfect alternative out there. The bad news is there's not one perfect system. They all have unintended negative consequences, yet I can confidently say that better solutions exist than our antiquated system.

Voting systems that remove the power from electors and legislators and back to the power of the people, where it should be.

One of the best alternatives is called "Proportional Ranked Choice Voting." This method is gaining traction in some states. It works by doing just what the title says; a portion of the vote is given to candidates based on their percentage of the vote instead of the "winner-take-all" scenario we have now.

So, if you're one of those 6+ million in California who voted for Trump and one of those 5.2 million Biden voters in Texas, you would have had your vote count in 2020 if we were using a proportional voting system.

Can you imagine how much more interest there would be in primaries and other voting elections if more people felt confident their vote would count?

There are other benefits to Ranked Choice Voting that most people don't know about. I'm an educator, so I'll use sophisticated emojis and compare the two systems to help my visual learners.

	Promotes Better Representation	Reduces Negative Campaigning	Provides More Choices	Minimizes Voting for "Lesser of Two Evils" Candidates
Current Electoral College System	😠	😠	😠	😠
Ranked Choice Voting	😇	😇	😇	😇

Two more thoughts about switching to a system like Proportional Ranked-Choice Voting:

First, it represents an imperfect yet improved voting system in the United States. Keep in mind all large democratic initiatives take time to improve. Most of our enduring social programs, which enjoy overwhelming support among Americans, like social security, encountered stiff resistance initially and have consistently evolved to enhance their effectiveness.

Ranked Choice Voting is increasingly being used for city and state elections, and you have a great opportunity to push it along in your state. This initiative has already been enacted amongst 12 historically Republican-leaning and Democratic states.

Do you believe we need to evolve away from our current system and more towards a system in which everyone's vote counts? Join the Ranked Choice Voting Reform in your state. The link is provided in the footnotes below.[52]

Are you passionate about passing the National Popular Vote Act? Join the Petition in Your State to Amend the Constitution via the National Popular Interstate Act.[53]

Ok… I have some great news… you have weathered the DARKEST part of this book. No more doom and gloom (ok, a little…but not like the YouTube videos you see where that guy dressed as a bush scares the hell out of unsuspecting people in the street).

Hope sometimes arrives in surprising, unexpected ways, and this is the subject of my next chapter.

I'm sure you've heard many inaccurate definitions of our youth, and I'm here to tell you that's BS. I've completed a lot of interviews for this book with a spectrum of young voters, and here's the great news: Today's youth is dialed into the modern world and dedicated to solving our democracy crisis, along with the world's other major problems like climate change.

---

52 https://www.fairvote.org/rcv#where_is_ranked_choice_voting_used

53 https://www.nationalpopularvote.com/

I mentioned in the introduction that getting involved with political reform may just be one of the most important things to bring meaning to your life. If you doubt that, let me introduce you to some of the most bright, passionate, informed, and intelligent examples of today's generation in the chapter ahead.

You'll hear their ideas of a better democracy, how they plan to fight for change, and how they epitomize the essence of what it means to be a citizen.

They are superheroes without a lot of superpowers… yet. And they need our help to make this happen.

Let's look at how you can join them and make seismic differences in future generations.

Chapter 5

Today's Generation: Mad as Hell and Begging Us to Prove Them Wrong

Vanessa Nakate, an 18-year-old climate activist, took the stage at the 2021 United Nations' Climate Talks and channeled a message that echoed the concerns of her generation: "Where I live (in Columbia), a 2-degree world means a billion people will be affected by heat stress. At that temperature, the human body cannot cool itself by sweating. Even healthy people sitting in the shade will die within 6 hours."

As Nakate looked at the audience filled with leaders who have over-promised and under-delivered on climate change, she begged for help. "I'm actually here to beg you to prove us wrong. We desperately need you to prove us wrong. Please prove us wrong. God, help us all if you fail to prove us wrong. God help us."[54]

"Prove us wrong." Vanessa delivered her impassioned plea to a room full of the world's most powerful leaders. Leaders who, with the stroke of a pen, could take swift action to curb emissions and

---

[54] Lisa Friedman and Alyssa Lukpat, "Vanessa Nakate, Speaking for a Leery Youth Movement, Offers a Challenge: 'Prove US Wrong.,'" The New York Times, November 11, 2021, https://www.nytimes.com/2021/11/11/climate/vanessa-nakate-speaking-for-a-leery-youth-movement-offers-a-challenge-prove-us-wrong.html?fbclid=IwAR16YETzIkO8O-qGiWYrlMZgOYAedUyao9Z5MdLehCsDQ5_W0K7MsHeULcA.

save our planet. Yet Vanessa's message was not limited to her. It also clearly echoed in the conversations I had with today's newest voting generations in the United States.

So why do our youth feel so unheard, and what do they have to say?

I've noticed older generations asserting that today's generation is out of touch with global issues, often attributing this perception to their seemingly constant phone use. However, I found in my interviews that this assumption is horribly inaccurate. I was utterly amazed by both their exceptional creativity and how articulate their suggestions were when asked about how to enhance US politics for their generation.

I believe this disconnect often occurs because we simply don't try to have meaningful dialogue and validate their perspectives. At times, we may not speak the language needed to connect with them.

Here's a simple test to prove they're watching and listening: Ask a young person if they use Facebook. The majority will likely tell you they avoid the platform due to their perception that it was ruined by adults. You may not be aware of this, but today's generation keeps their preferred social media platforms a secret, seeking an escape from their parents due to the concerns above. (Plus, who really wants to see your parents kissing on Facebook? Ewww.)

So, what did they have to say about US politics in my interviews?

In general, many believe adults do not know how to discuss politics effectively with each other.

They watched in dismay as their parents engaged in childlike arguments over the great mask debate, which led them to believe that constructive political discussions were beyond reach.

Many felt that their generation are now the ones on the hook to combat the issue after their parents and politicians failed to grasp the seriousness of the problem.

The thought by some older adults that the younger generations don't watch the news appears to be inaccurate. They just don't use the same platforms.

A 2021 poll by the American Press Institute found that 79% of Generation Z reads the news daily, poking holes in the theory that this generation is tuned out.[55] They are more tuned in than older generations give them credit for, and they are far more skeptical of traditional news stories. I'd say they're pretty intuitive. (And yes, they also sometimes tune us out.)

I felt a genuine sense of sadness as I listened to some of their responses explaining why they were disheartened by the state of our nation.

You only need to review the Sandy Hook school shooting in 2012 to see what shapes their perspective and how much of the rhetoric we watch on television or online can spiral out of control.

During this horrific event, an active shooter mercilessly claimed the lives of 26 young individuals, marking one of the most dreadful tragedies in recent memory. Yet afterward, a group of "adults" abandoned this reality and chose to monetize a conspiracy theory that called the shooting a hoax.[56]

---

55 The Media Insight Project, "The News Consumption Habits of 16- to 40-Year-Olds," American Press Institute, August 31, 2022, https://www.americanpressinstitute.org/publications/reports/survey-research/the-news-consumption-habits-of-16-to-40-year-olds/.

56 Dave Collins, "Alex Jones Ordered to Pay $473m More to Sandy Hook Families," AP News, November 10, 2022, https://apnews.com/article/entertainment-shootings-business-connecticut-alex-jones-c6d0563dc17e7bfa83a881b44e7b9eec.

This would have been a perfect time to unite the country and finally have real conversations about gun safety, but again we failed and let our youth down. Sure, politicians offered "thoughts and prayers" after the tragedy, but little was changed despite calls for more effective gun laws.

Many young people feel as though they are stuck in a "national crisis" time loop. It's like a horror movie version of "Groundhog Day," in which parents, political pundits, and politicians argue over whose fault it was instead of coming together to solve this problem. The madness continues when everyone seems to forget about the incident until the next tragedy occurs.

This isn't politics as normal – this is a battlefield using our children as pawns.

So, what has all this infighting and Hatfield and McCoy style standoffs on Facebook and Twitter over masks, "freedoms," "rights," and other political battles done to our children?

A 2021 Harvard Youth poll offers insight into the fact that our youth are in very deep trouble. More than 50% of the 2,513 survey respondents aged 18-29 said they felt "down, depressed, or hopeless." A heart-breaking 28% said they felt 'better off dead'.

When I first read this poll, I was in a coffee shop in Phoenix, Arizona, writing this book. I had to re-read the results several times. My mind wouldn't allow me to accept the data that was written. I just kept reading the poll repeatedly in disbelief, thinking I had misread it. I then had to accept the data for what it was. The enormity of this situation brought tears to my eyes right there in the restaurant.

It was also my motivation for writing this book, my *aha* moment, my ikigai purpose, to help today's generation improve the world they live in. ("Ikigai" is a Japanese word that refers to a passion that gives someone value and joy to life.)

There is no silver lining to the poll above, yet I can tell you with 100% certainty from doing hundreds of interviews that our youth are resilient. They are strong, bright, funny, and intelligent.

They want change, and they want it now. They are mad, angry, and mobilizing. They don't really seem to care if you're a Republican, Democrat, Independent, or any other political label. They are *desperate* for positive change and unity at both the local and global levels.

What they want most of all, though, is just for us to listen, unplug, and help them navigate a world that seems to be increasingly crashing down upon them.

I mentioned earlier this newest voting generation is full of inspiration. Let me offer another example of a modern-day world changer.

In 2018, Emma Gonzales, then an 18-year-old student at Marjory Stoneman Douglas High School, the scene of another mass school shooting, organized one of the largest youth protests since the Vietnam War.

Emma's call to action included a scolding for adults. "Every single person up here today, all these people should be home grieving. Instead, we are up here standing together because if all our government and president can do is send thoughts and prayers, then it's time for the victims to be the change that we need to see.[57]"

My interviews clearly revealed that the current generation struggles to comprehend why we're so bad at uniting to effect positive change.

---

[57] Taylor, Kate. "America's Teenagers Skew a Lot More Conservative than Most People Realize, and They Get Most of Their News from Instagram." Business Insider. Accessed August 25, 2023. https://www.businessinsider.com/gen-z-changes-political-divides-2019-7.

So what did my interviews show about today's youth, and what are their concerns? And what types of changes are important to them?

- Election reforms
- Less focus on political labels. More than 50% do not see themselves as conservative or liberal.
- More focus on climate change (almost universal agreement)
- Legalized marijuana (almost universal agreement)
- Gun rights with pragmatic gun control[58]
- Better awareness of mental health issues.

Most do not see themselves as liberal or conservative. They are breaking up with politics in record numbers, so we have got to *stop treating them like they want the same things politically as we do*. They are generally more in tune with today's modern woes and ready to tackle them head-on.

After my interviews, I realized this generation, which many discard because of their constant cell phone use, has a lot to teach us.

For example, my wife's son is an activist in his 20s with a degree in Environmental Sustainability. Listening to him has significantly expanded my understanding of environmental issues. I draw strength from his unwavering dedication to preserving a world that strives to ensure its survival for future generations.

Another observation from my interviews is that this newest generation has a strong BS indicator. They can easily discern the rhetoric when politicians and influencers promote their agenda. They want genuine answers.

---

[58] Nadeem, Reem. "Amid a Series of Mass Shootings in the U.S., Gun Policy Remains Deeply Divisive." Pew Research Center - U.S. Politics & Policy, April 28, 2022. https://www.pewresearch.org/politics/2021/04/20/amid-a-series-of-mass-shootings-in-the-u-s-gun-policy-remains-deeply-divisive/.

That gets us back to a call to action. Let's *prove them wrong*. We are a resilient country. We help strangers we don't even know in times of crisis and, for the most part, do the right thing when it comes to helping our neighbors.

I want to personally thank those who offered their time and energy before I offer some feedback below from interviews I conducted with our newest voting generations (mostly 18-30 years old). Your input was courageous, genuine, and amazing. It opened my eyes to what we should work towards instead of what we're trying to repair.

Many young people are frustrated by the lack of progress in today's democracy. They may believe adults don't want to hear their pleas for change. But some adults are listening and witnessing the world they're trying to shape.

Many of the participant's answers on how to improve the path of our democracy are not mainstream. Many of their insights do not match the same answers older generations hear on their favorite cable network.

Let's read about some of these changes our newest voters have expressed:

Election Reform

My findings show that almost 85% of respondents want change in how we elect our local officials and presidents. Many answered that they thought Ranked Choice Voting would provide, at the very least, a stepping stone to a better system. The idea of an election conspiracy was far from my mind as a new voter in the 1980s. I didn't even know what the term *gerrymandering* meant, yet unfortunately, it seems like this reality is now part of the voting experience for our newest voting generations.

One participant answered, "Access to voting and the nature of our elections are in many cases being shaped by a conspiracy. Relative representation is skewed in many states via gerrymandering."

Other voting reform ideas from my participants included:

- **Adopting a one-day "winner take all" Presidential primary**. Currently, the presidential primary system is a drawn-out, tiring, marathon that begins as soon as the first candidate throws their hat in the ring announcing their candidacy (in 2016 the first candidate announced his presidency with 596 days until the election!)[59]

  This lengthy marathon leaves us voters weary from the countless commercials watching the candidates mercilessly attack each other on TV. This marathon is not healthy for the public or candidates.

  Some of my participants felt having a one-day "winner take all" presidential primary would not only eliminate this ugliness but also reduce the advantages that some candidates receive because they have a larger financial war chest.

  They point to the fact that candidates more popular with their generation had to drop out due to the lack of prevailing votes after Joe Biden gained momentum to win the nomination in the 2020 Presidential election.

  Bite-Sized Learning:
  Both parties, unfortunately, try to influence who wins the election. For example, the Democratic Party purposely

[59] Danielle Kurtzleben, "Why Are U.S. Elections so Much Longer than Other Countries'?," NPR, October 21, 2015, https://www.npr.org/sections/itsallpolitics/2015/10/21/450238156/canadas-11-week-campaign-reminds-us-that-american-elections-are-much-longer.

moved more primaries into conservative blue-leaning states for the *Super Tuesday* primary in 1984. Their goal was to elect a more moderate candidate after Walter Mondale lost big to Ronald Reagan that year. This ultimately backfired after the next Democratic candidate, Governor Michael Dukakis, also lost badly in 1988.[60]

- **End legalized bribery of politicians (dark money).** Most voters, including Generation Z, believe that large corporations influence politics. Yet many people don't fully understand just how much control these corporations have.

  My participants had an even wider knowledge of just how damaging it is. Some of the participants I interviewed are behind the "Represent Us Act" to end corporate influence on what legislature gets passed and what doesn't.

  Bite-Sized Learning:
  A 2014 Princeton Study found "the preferences of the average American appear to have had a minuscule, near-zero… impact on public policy". Even if 80% of us agree on an issue, the chance of something becoming law is only near 30%. However, if you can afford a lobbyist, that percentage dramatically changes, up to nearly 60%. And guess who ends up paying for this loss of representation? You and I.[61]

- **Reforming the House of Representatives** to better represent population changes in the United States. This was another suggested proposal that my much younger, and wiser at times, participants felt offered reform to help better represent them.

---

[60] Montanaro, Domenico. "Super Tuesday Was Created to Nominate Someone Moderate. It Backfired." NPR, March 1, 2020. https://www.npr.org/2016/02/29/468253626/a-history-of-super-tuesday.

[61] https://www.youtube.com/watch?v=5tu32CCA_Ig&t=6s

The number of people represented by one U.S. House membership has grown from 57,169 to a whopping 747,184 in 2018. Given the dismal numbers that offer insight into public trust and representation in government, this renovation seems like a positive reform.[62] Danielle Allen, a political theorist at Harvard University writes, "Our institutions weren't meant for this - and we've been cobbling on additions and extensions decade after decade.[63]"

Bite-Size Learning:
Our Representatives currently represent about 760,000 people in their district. You read that number correctly. Having too large of representation adds to voter inequality, and gerrymandering, and is a horrible violation of the 'one-person-one-vote' pillar of democracy. Studies show not feeling represented properly is one of the primary reasons people rebel, and this poor representation just adds to the belief that our current representational democracy is sliding into dangerous territory.

Our Founding Fathers never intended for this number to bloat this high. This number is 15 times larger than the maximum size of 50,000 proposed by the first Congress.[64]

One solution would be to increase the number of Representatives to approximately 6,600 (or 1 Representative

---

62 Peter Bell, "Public Trust in Government: 1958-2022," Pew Research Center - U.S. Politics & Policy, August 22, 2023, https://www.pewresearch.org/politics/2022/06/06/public-trust-in-government-1958-2022/.

63 Allen, Danielle. "Opinion | The House Was Supposed to Grow with Population. It Didn't. Let's Fix That." The Washington Post, August 23, 2023. https://www.washingtonpost.com/opinions/2023/02/28/danielle-allen-democracy-reform-congress-house-expansion/.

64 "Learn How We Can Replace Career Politicians with Citizen Legislators by Enlarging the U.S. House of Representatives.," Thirty-Thousand, August 12, 2022, https://thirty-thousand.org/overview/.

for approximately every 50,000 citizens) to give us more equal representation. I asked one of my participants how they'd ever fit this many people into the House of Representatives. His answer? "How many Zoom calls have you been on lately?" I smiled. Yes, modern technology would allow this idea to work.

Do you want to add your name to the list of individuals who are determined to return the People's House back to the people? I've put resources in the footnotes for those who want to learn more about how to contact your State Senator to support the Equal Voices Act.[65]

Review this graph to see how the amount of people represented by our lawmakers compares to the number of people represented by other democracies around the world.

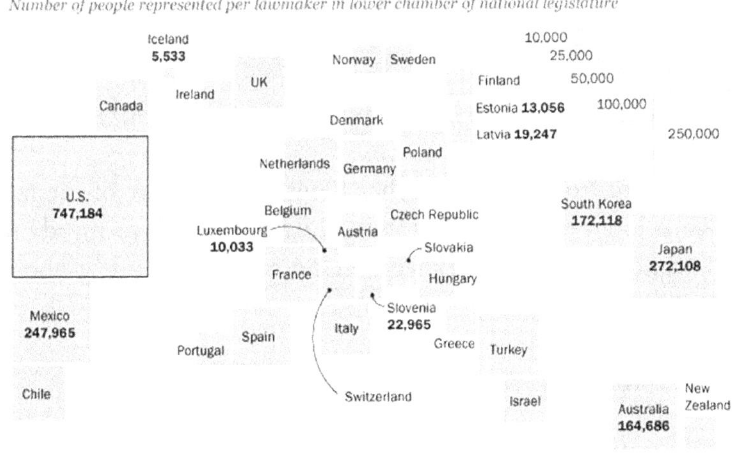

(Source: Pew Research Center)

[65] https://thirty-thousand.org/overview/ or https://www.congress.gov/bill/118th-congress/house-bill/643?q=%7B%22search%22%3A%5B%22casten%22%5D%7D&s=2&r=24

One of the key takeaways I hope you take from this book is that working to enhance our democracy is not a futile endeavor.

Let me prove it.

There are numerous issues that once seemed unreachable until most citizens decided to change. A change in one state eventually leads to changes in other states until the majority have enacted fairer laws that reflect the true will of the people.

I've included a great video to show you just how this works, from grassroots campaigns like the ones our newest voters want (see footnote for link).[66] For example, almost 9 out of 10 people support the idea of reforming dark money. Dozens of states have already enacted reform policies to help us regain control of where power belongs – in the people's hands. In fact, by the time you read this, more states will have enacted these common-sense laws. When this tipping point occurs, more and more states enact similar laws. That's how change occurs and why it gives me hope that our democracy isn't dead yet.

So, what else can we do to better support our democracy?

The statement from Martin Luther King, Jr., "The arc of the moral universe is long, but it bends toward justice," comes to mind. Yet I would argue that the arc he's referencing is usually bent by those in power.

And that's where you can help.

The next approach I'm about to propose to support our youth sometimes makes people uneasy - kind of like that feeling when you're not sure if you should enter an already crowded elevator (maybe that's just me?). But here's the uncomfortable truth: We may

---

[66] https://youtu.be/UTP4uvIFu5c

have good intentions to help our youth create a better world, yet intentions without power are just good intentions.

We already know that our young adults are superheroes to survive in this day and age. What they lack, though…is the *power to change it.*

There are three irrefutable truths regarding power: First, those who have it rarely give it up without a fight.

Second, power unchecked can become unbelievably destructive. I'm sure you know leaders who used their power to create unspeakable crimes against humanity fueled by their less-than-holy vision of a distorted reality. You've already read about the many "leaders" (like Mussolini or Hitler, among many others) who yielded so much power that they destroyed entire generations in their quest for some less-than-holy vision of a distorted reality.

The third irrefutable law of power is this: Power is just energy, and that energy decides whether it is used as a destructive force, like we saw on January 6th, or used for good.

When we harness political power in the right ways, it can have a great impact on current and future generations. Let's look at a case in which political authority was used for universal good: the creation of social security.

More than 90% of Americans believe social security was one of the most important social initiatives of the 20th century.[67] Still, it took power to make it a reality.

Before The Great Depression, there were very few public programs to protect the nation's elderly. Many lived in destitution, and during

[67] "AARP Poll Finds 96 Percent Support Social Security ." AARP, August 24, 2022. https://www.aarp.org/retirement/social-security/info-2020/aarp-poll-finds-near-universal-support.html.

the great depression, 50% lived in poverty, relying primarily on local charities and their family for basic living conditions.[68]

When The Great Depression occurred, our nation's most vulnerable population, many of whom had fought in World War I, became even more destitute.

Americans demanded government intervention, and in 1935, the first step towards helping our elderly receive a better living was enacted. Like most social programs, Social Security has undergone many changes, but it still provides a safety net for this group of citizens in the United States. Most would agree the Social Security Act of 1935 has vastly improved our elderly's living conditions.

This is what I mean by power. Power is energy. This energy is harnessed for either positive or negative purposes when a critical mass of individuals clamor for change.

This brings us to today and our youth. Our youth need us; they want a better America, but they lack power. *They are superheroes without a lot of superpowers*. So, let's work on getting them more power.

But how do we do this? Passion…and a little direction.

I discovered that using a set of guiding questions provided me with a roadmap that effectively channeled my passions when determining my most compelling areas of focus for social change.

I've been a social activist since I was in my teens. Yet I know that many people don't feel called to a life in activism. I've witnessed a growing number of individuals, perhaps like you, increasingly eager to correct the course of our tilting ship, displaying a willingness

[68] Veghte, Benjamin. "Social Security's Past, Present and Future." National Academy of Social Insurance – Advancing Solutions for Social Security, Medicare, and Medicaid, November 30, 2020. https://www.nasi.org/discussion/social-securitys-past-present-and-future/.

to step forward and play their part in securing a better future for upcoming generations - “the times they are a-changin’,” as our good friend, Bob Dylan, would tell us.

Here’s a great exercise to help narrow your interests for those of you who may be new activists.

This checklist below is also available for printing and in soft copy form on our website.[69]

Checklist for Activists:

1. What issues are you most passionate about?
2. If you could change the problem, what would the positive results create?
3. How do we get there? Some solutions may include:
    a. Writing your state senators and congressional representatives to voice your concerns, why they’re important, and what you’d like them to do to change the problem.
    b. Writing an Op-Ed (an editorial opinion you write to your city newspaper or national news sources like the New York Post and Times). Note: This is a great one for any young adult, as these letters have no age restriction!
    c. Starting a blog. This is an easy way to get your voice heard and connect with others to promote action.
    d. Joining online communities. This is perhaps the easiest way to connect with others who are passionate about the same cause. For example, I started the subreddit “Revolution Without the R” to connect with others who want to discuss large, non-partisan ways to affect changes in the United States political system.

[69] http://www.coachingforevolution.com

e. Speaking at city council meetings. Politicians may not listen well, but they do listen when there are enough people who are passionate about an issue. Nothing says power more than numbers.
f. Start your own group. This is as easy as starting a Meetup Group or a Facebook site dedicated to your cause. For example, I'm in a Meetup group working on a letter-writing campaign to change Arizona's current archaic voting system.

I hope this chapter has made you slightly more positive about how democratic change in America can happen and, better yet, how you can support those who will most likely be affected by your support.

I believe there are enough of us who want to lay down our ceremonial swords and stop battling against each other.

Americans are some of the most generous people in the world, and at our core is that strength.

We saw this in the wake of 9/11 as thousands of us rescued brick by brick those caught in the rubble. You'll see our true spirit after floods when neighbors help neighbors pack sandbags to help save their community. They're not worried about saving a "Democratic" or "Republican" neighbor. They're there to help a human being.

We'll tackle some of the biggest barriers preventing our true colors from showing. You'll see in the next chapter that science shows we have very little defense against the mediums fueling our discontent and the possibility of another civil war. We'll also discuss one of the deadliest concerns that can put our country into a democracy death spiral.

Let's check out our next chapter and learn from experts on how you can modify your social media world for a better online experience while at the same time making a dent in the toxic online hate that causes division.

Chapter 6:

Emojis Against Humanity: How Social Media May Be Fueling the Next Civil War

What happens to our brains when we read something on social media that catches our interest?

To explain this, I'm going to introduce you to a conspiracy we can all agree on... *The Birds Aren't Real* conspiracy. It was created by my favorite conspiracist, Peter McIndoe. Yes, this is a real story, so feel free to Google it, and I'll see you again in about 20 minutes. (By the way, this chapter also discusses how we can defend ourselves against random clickbait.)

So, let's see what happens to your brain when you read about something new.

It's 7 pm. You're ready to finally start that important work project you've been dreading when you receive a text from your friend saying, "Have you seen this? Is it real?" along with a link to a story.

Earlier in the day, you caught the tail-end of a snippet on the internet about some guy claiming birds were dropping from the sky and simultaneously being replaced with bird drones. These "bird drones" are now spying on unsuspecting citizens from above. You dismissed it as nonsense (as you should), but now your friend's text has you curious.

You click on the link, and sure enough, there seems to be proof that some dark agency is replacing our beaked friends with actual drones. You think to yourself, "What the hell, that can't be right, is it?" Your prefrontal cortex goes into action. Our brains tend to view new information as preferable to the old truths we once knew. This means that our attention can be hijacked by this fresh data fairly quickly.[70]

You turn on the REAL news, CNN and Fox, to see if it has hit the national airwaves yet.

Politician Larry Left is battling it out with Senator Rachel Wright on Fox News, saying that she can't believe the current administration didn't do enough to stop this bird takeover. Not convinced of the validity yet, you decide to switch channels to see what CNN has to say. CNN presents a story defending Larry Left, explaining that the previous administration knew about it but chose to cover it up.

Now, you don't know what to believe. In your quest for more information, you decide to turn to X (formerly Twitter). Thousands

---

[70] Daniel J. Levitin. Extracted from The Organized Mind: Thinking Straight in the Age of Information Overload, published by Viking.

of people on Twitter fuel the proof that this indeed did occur as is being reported.

You look up at the clock, and it's now 9:30 p.m. Oh crap! You forgot about the project. Well, go to work tomorrow with your head held high and blame the birds.

Did you actually go to the internet and check out this story before returning to this book? If so, your brain was doing just what it was intended to do: find out the truth so you can see how you should respond to novelty. Some of this isn't your fault. We often get caught up in a dopamine-addicted feedback loop, effectively rewarding our brain for losing focus.

This was a comical way of describing what happens to our brains when we mindlessly scroll on the internet or try to find facts on cable television that support a sensational story. (You've been warned about these diabolical birds fitted with cameras – "if it flies, it spies").

You've also read why we sometimes go down that rabbit hole. More information is supposed to be good for us, right? Yet, according to Neuroscientist Michael J. Levitin's book, "Why the Modern World is Bad for Your Brain," we just can't maneuver that well when we're in multitasking mode. Long-term effects of this information overload include anxiety, irritability, difficulty sleeping, and mood swings. We don't just feel mentally tired. We *are* physically and mentally exhausted.[71]

Unfortunately, cable news, paid influencers, and talk-show hosts also know about this new misinformation weapon and how our brains thirst for unique stories. And it's big business for them. It's also a dangerous way to push dark, ideological theories that threaten democracy.

---

[71] Levitin.

You may think we all have cognitive weapons that help us separate fact from fiction yet converting someone from a normal citizen to a full-blown, conspiracy-believing American is occurring at an astonishing level.

Let's look at how quick it takes for one of these journeys from normalcy to dangerous extremism.

Carol Smith was a new Facebook user in 2019. Like everyone else, she listed her interests when creating her profile so Facebook could offer stories that better matched her interests.

Carol described herself as a "conservative mom." After liking a few mainstream pages that matched her interests, Facebook's algorithms began sending her conspiracy content they believed would interest her. Even though in her interests she didn't follow QAnon, within 5 days, she began receiving invitations to join groups with ties to QAnon. One was from a group stating how white genocide was occurring.

Now, here's the real story: Facebook "Carol" was really a Facebook employee turned whistleblower who was troubled by how quickly someone would start receiving dangerous conspiracy information like this.

Timberg, Dwoskin, and Albergotti concluded in their article, "Inside Facebook, Jan. 6 Violence Fueled Anger, Regret over Missed Warning Signs," that "the content in this account devolved to a quite troubling, polarizing, state in an extremely short period of time.[72]"

---

[72] Craig Timberg, Elizabeth Dwoskin, and Reed Albergotti, "Inside Facebook, Jan. 6 Violence Fueled Anger, Regret over Missed Warning Signs," The Washington Post, October 29, 2021, https://www.washingtonpost.com/technology/2021/10/22/jan-6-capitol-riot-facebook/.

Not taking these alarm bells seriously was nothing new, as Facebook whistleblower Frances Haugen testified in Congress in 2021 and on the US news program "60 Minutes."

Testifying before Congress, Haugen stated, "During my time at Facebook, I came to realize a devastating truth: Almost no one outside of Facebook knows what happens inside Facebook." The problem wasn't that Facebook didn't know about the problems, which led users down rabbit holes. The problem was that upper management seemed to ignore the gravity of the issue. In fact, the Facebook group meant to harness toxic content on the platform was simply disbanded after the 2020 election. It was as if they were doing a victory lap and absolving themselves of any responsibility simultaneously. They (perhaps rightly) assumed that everyone would forget about their toxic algorithms after the next news cycle.

You would think most of the larger social media platforms would be taking their role more seriously after the January 6th insurrection. Yet there are still massive potholes in their road to recovery.

Here's what is clear: Facebook researchers warned us about fueling dangerous conspiracy content in 2019, a full year before the insurrection. In fact, Facebook allowed dangerous QAnon influencers to operate unchecked for over a year before its first attempted crackdown.[73]

I want to explain why sharing misinformation is so dangerous.

According to scientists Bunzek and Duzel, we have an innate neurological reflex to seek unique knowledge, and a very good reason why we seek this information - it makes us happy.[74]

---

[73] Timberg, 2021

[74] Nico Bunzeck and Emrah Düzel, "Absolute Coding of Stimulus Novelty in the Human Substantia Nigra/VTA," Neuron, August 2, 2006, https://www.sciencedirect.com/science/article/pii/S0896627306004752.

If most of that information comes from that crazy cousin who posts it on Facebook, we can easily separate this fact from fiction. Yet our reality becomes skewed when we trust the sources of that material because that misinformation becomes our reality. This mind trick is called "Authority Bias," and this bias is seen frequently in revolts.

The second reason this mass misinformation is so dangerous is its ability to speed up the journey from normalcy to extremism.

But why does this occur in some people in such a rapid amount of time?

Let's turn to the Center for BrainHealth at the University of Texas for some answers.

Dr. Chapman, Ph.D., writes, "Social media... is a curated version of the world in a way that the algorithms think the user's brain wants to see it. This can have a profound impact because what the user reads and writes on a screen…shapes how your brain processes and gathers information.[75]"

So social media and biased newspapers not only describe the world we live in, but they also help create our reality.

We join online communities to help us connect with like-minded individuals. But what if those online communities are dangerous? It's no secret that terrorist networks use sites to recruit others, and it should not be surprising that many of the people convicted in the January 6th insurrection credited Facebook groups for uniting them.

Why I believe it's so serious, and should be named a public health threat, is how *quickly* it can influence someone to become polarized.

---

75 Harris Eyre, Ian MacRae, and Sandi Chapman, "Social Media Is Changing Our Brains," Center for BrainHealth® The University of Texas at Dallas, December 5, 2021, https://centerforbrainhealth.org/article/social-media-is-changing-our-brains.

This spells trouble for democracy and adds just another factor that could contribute to a civil war or other uprisings.

We just learned that we're not powerless against this hate, so why does it occur? Let's learn a little about The Horns Effect (the evil cousin of the cognitive bias trait called "The Halo Effect").

The Horns Effect states our negative cognitive bias causes an adverse impression of someone or something, even if it is incorrect. This effect shows up in ways we may not even be aware of, like in the employment hiring process, when we think about political candidates, and even in healthcare.

But just why should we be so worried about the rise of damaging social media effects? In many neuroscientists' minds, it is Public Health Risk #1. We just haven't identified it as this yet.

I can see many of you shrugging your shoulders or rolling your eyes (no, I don't have a hidden camera somewhere in this book). You may say, "It's just social media." That may be true, but how many times have you caught yourself endlessly sifting through meaningless stories, and 30 minutes later, you've wondered why you burnt dinner? Or a story's ability to make you angry?

Remember, at one time, cigarette smoking wasn't thought of as dangerous either.

Let's look at something that appeared seemingly harmless when it was introduced and how it was used to manipulate us.

In 2016, Facebook added additional emojis, which were widely accepted by its users. These included the "love," "haha," "wow," "sad," and "angry" icons.

Now, you would think these well-intentioned additions were harmless, right? If you thought, "Most people wouldn't be influenced by these new Facebook family members," you're partly right. But that's where the story goes terribly wrong.

Facebook's researchers soon discovered there was a "critical flaw" in which the new *angry* icon received much more attention than the other newly introduced icons.

This accidental discovery helped Facebook intentionally push more emotional and provocative content. The theory was that "posts that prompted lots of reaction… tended to keep users more engaged". Guess what more engagement meant? You got it… dollars (insert smiling emoji for Facebook executives here).

The new *angry* icon was almost like a gateway drug for some users. This negative content was also disproportionately linked to "misinformation, toxicity, and low-quality news.[76]"

Using algorithms to manipulate people's emotions may not be illegal, but it is unethical. Meta claims to have ceased this practice, but there is evidence that it was a factor in the Insurrection and other events.

Let's examine additional factors that are causing concern from *Revolution Analysts* like myself. I call this next section "Politicians Behaving Badly."

Before I get started, though, I'm going to hit you with a shocking statement: At times, politicians will say things that may not be accurate and/or to help them get elected. I know, I know, that statement is difficult to believe. But are there times when politicians knowingly say things to promote violence or lead to violence?

---

[76] Jeremy B. Merrill and Will Oremus, "Five Points for Anger, One for a 'like': How Facebook's Formula Fostered Rage and Misinformation," The Washington Post, October 26, 2021, https://www.washingtonpost.com/technology/2021/10/26/facebook-angry-emoji-algorithm/.

The answer, unsurprisingly, is yes. And this occurs on both sides of the political fence.

We already know that the January 6th trial has shown the very real effects of what misinformation may cause. In the Introduction, you read about Stephen Ayres, a January 6th protestor turned Capitol invader, and his testimony about how he thought the message coming from the "Stop the Steal" organizers meant it was time to "stand up to tyranny."

Yet the insurrection has done little to stop some politicians from using inflammatory language to divide us and motivate their base to believe the other side is the enemy. You've probably heard one politician say something that made the hairs on the back of your neck stand up. But is this political fire branding any worse than it was even 10 years ago?

The answer is yes, and it is one of the causes that have so badly divided us. Politicians understand the equation, as well as our major news outlets and social media.

In an article titled "The Mean Tweets Are Coming from Inside The House. Study Of Politicians' Twitter Looks at 'Civility,'" Rep. Ted Lieu stated, "What I found is in the last five years, when the former President (Trump) would say something… false, and I responded to that, that would get higher engagement.[77]" Consequently, he would highlight anything false he believed Trump would say.

Cambridge University Press found that "tweet negativity and overall rate of tweeting increases as the campaign season progresses.[78]"

---

[77] Mason, Melanie. "The Mean Tweets Are Coming from inside the House. Study of Politicians' Twitter Looks at 'Civility.'" Los Angeles Times, April 28, 2022. https://www.latimes.com/politics/story/2022-04-28/twitter-incivility-up-among-members-of-congress-study-finds.

[78] Justin H. Gross and Kaylee T. Johnson, "Twitter Taunts and Tirades: Negative Campaigning in the Age of Trump: PS: Political Science

We may be finding one of the primary root causes of our political divide.

According to a Pew Research poll, 85% of those surveyed say that the tone and nature of political debate have become more negative over the last several years. This same poll revealed that 78% of instances where heated or aggressive is used to discuss specific individuals or groups can increase the likelihood of violence against them.[79]

Remember earlier when we read that uprisings contain both a social and a political element to them?

Revolutions do not occur overnight; they are like embers in a slow-moving fire. They appear after long periods of distrust and the inability of political leaders to show compromise. Finally, a spark appears in the shape of an event along with other factors like an economic depression, and the uprising takes root.

We're beginning to learn some habits and strategies to fight misinformation better and take back our social media experience. And in our next chapter, you'll learn how to battle back against these powerful dopamine-induced headlines.

& Politics," Cambridge Core, October 12, 2016, https://www.cambridge.org/core/journals/ps-political-science-and-politics/article/abs/twitter-taunts-and-tirades-negative-campaigning-in-the-age-of-trump/D9EFBAABAE89FB0F64DD24B6DA049E89.

[79] Bruce Drake and Jocelyn Kiley, "Americans Say the Nation's Political Debate Has Grown More Toxic and 'heated' Rhetoric Could Lead to Violence," Pew Research Center, May 28, 2021, https://www.pewresearch.org/short-reads/2019/07/18/americans-say-the-nations-political-debate-has-grown-more-toxic-and-heated-rhetoric-could-lead-to-violence/.

Chapter 7

Breaking Up With (Harmful) Media… It's Not You. It's Them

As the wave of "patriots" armed with guns, weapons, and malice tore through Capitol Police lines on January 6th, 18-year-old Jackson Reffitt made a phone call no son should ever have to make: turning in his father, Guy Reffitt, to the FBI.

Guy Reffitt's story from mainstream citizens to is eerily similar to those arrested after the insurrection that day, like Stephen Ayres, who testified at the January 6th Committee.

Guy had earned good money at one time in his life, making as much as $30,000 per month. This amount allowed Guy to take care of his family, sending all three of their children to private school and living in a penthouse with a view of the ocean while working as a contractor in Malaysia. Times were good for Guy, yet like any other economic cycle, good times don't last forever, and a decline in the oil industry was about to change his family's life forever.

As the price of oil plummeted, the family moved from Malaysia to Texas, and the once-cherished prosperity they enjoyed ended with a thud. Guy's wife Nicole confesses, "We had no money, literally. I don't know what happened, but we really didn't end up saving any money." The family went from living the good life in penthouses to living on an air mattress with no TV.

A common person found in many rebellions includes individuals who had previously enjoyed a comfortable lifestyle and then suffered psychological loss of status in their lives.

Guy's son Jackson recalls his father's transition from normalcy to extremism as his family's bad times continued. His father was always interested in politics but felt him slide down the rabbit hole of extremism sometime after 2020. "Fox News… grew into Newsmax. And then he'd be on his Wiley Confederate page on Facebook."

Jackson did his best to gain a perspective of his father's view but to no avail. Over time, his angry outbursts became volatile.

Jackson claims his father's paranoia reached new heights with more involvement in these groups. His father began stockpiling weapons, ammo, and water. Guy had bought into the wild conspiracy idea that the electrical power grid would be shut down and the electoral votes would reset after the 2020 election.

His father began "patrolling" at riots and found shared ideals and community in groups like the Three-Percenters. (This group advocates gun ownership rights and resistance to the U.S. Government.)

His father consistently bragged about "doing something big" to help the cause.

Then, during the summer of 2020, Guy did something that deeply rattled Jackson and his family. While they were outside on the patio, Jackson's mother walked out and revealed that Guy had put a gun to her head. (Guy Reffitt denies these allegations.)[80]

---

80 Taki Telonidis and Brett Myers, "A Family Divided over Jan. 6: 'Traitors Get Shot,'" Reveal, January 17, 2023, https://revealnews.org/podcast/a-family-divided-over-jan-6-traitors-get-shot-2022/.

The weight of these matters pressed down on Jackson until he felt he could no longer bear it. Convinced that his father was now a threat to both his country and family, he made the fateful decision to contact the FBI.

Meanwhile, this "something big" Guy was bragging about earlier was foreshadowing for the January 6th rally in Washington, D.C.

Jackson recalls his mother revealing that their father was at the rally while the family watched from the living room television with obvious concern and disbelief.

Ironically, the FBI contacted Jackson as his family continued to watch the day's events unfold on January 6th. "Your timing is impeccable," Jackson said to his FBI contact. There would be no turning back for Jackson after that first contact with the FBI.

Jackson recalls being relieved to see his father return after attending the rally. Yet, this relief soon turned to fright.

The Reffitt family huddled in the kitchen, watching the nightly news as journalists reported the emerging details of the rally. There were reports of family members and friends identifying insurrectionists and turning them into the authorities.

Guy took this time to sternly warn Jackson and his sister, "If this ever happens, you'll ruin the family. You'll ruin what I was doing." His father's threat went one step further: "You know what happens to traitors? Traitors get shot."

Days later, the FBI barged through the Reffitt's door with AR-16s pointed at them.

Jackson's sister, Sarah, deduced that Jackson had been the family member who revealed their father's involvement after watching what the FBI removed as evidence from the home. "His computer was the only one they didn't take. They took all the computers in the house. Just not Jackson's."

Sarah also noted the caretaker role Jackson seemed to assume during the raid. As the FBI led his father away, she could overhear Jackson reassuring his mother, "Don't worry, Mom, everything's going to be fine. That's been the plan from the beginning."

History will show that Guy's prediction of "doing something big" was correct. He was one of the first insurrectionists to push through the police barricade and the first person prosecuted for his role in storming the Capitol on January 6th.

For the Reffitts, the future is uncertain at best, and this is only one example of the fallout from January 6th. Capitol police officers who lost their lives as a result of the insurrection paid the ultimate price. Other officers still deal with the psychological toll that day imprinted on them.

Let's take a look at the causes of what's driving the political anxiety you may be feeling now. You are not alone if you've kept your distance from selected friends and family members due to their political beliefs. Families have been torn apart by their political beliefs for some time now.

There are additional factors that you may not be aware of that contribute to this stress.

For example, the World Health Organization estimates that 25% of us suffer some type of generalized anxiety or depression brought on by a world turned upside down by COVID-19.[81] Those are

[81] Allison Brunier, "Covid-19 Pandemic Triggers 25% Increase in Prevalence of Anxiety and Depression Worldwide," World Health Organization, accessed August 27, 2023, https://www.who.int/news/item/02-03-2022-covid-19-pandemic-triggers-25-increase-in-prevalence-of-anxiety-and-depression-worldwide.

huge numbers, and we may not understand the exact toll that this pandemic has made on our psychological health until future studies reveal their findings.

Earlier in this book, I wrote that if we're going to heal America, some of that healing must start with you. I call it 'healing America from the inside out".

In Neuro Linguistic Program training, we practice a mindset to train ourselves to seek positive things. The mental toll of COVID-19, combined with everyday stresses and political upheaval, has increased demand for this type of training.

The mindset training can be summed up in the phrase, "What you focus on expands."

The same goes for having a relationship with social media. We can't expect it to change. Sure, most internet sites out there have group rules protecting people from hate speech and other toxicity, and some sites manage the space pretty well. The problem is that too many sites aren't managed well. We can't rely on 100% of the internet to play nice online. When money is at stake, they aren't going to police themselves for the greater good.

I want to introduce you to Dr. Samantha Boardman, a New York-based positive psychiatrist with one of the best prescriptions for creating a healthy relationship with social media. Her advice: forget *critical thinking* and instead focus on *critical ignoring*[82].

What? I know what you're thinking. It's been ingrained in us to pay attention in school, at work, while driving (that's probably good), and in 1-1 conversations. That still holds true, but not in the online battle to survive social media death-scrolling.

---

82 Anastasia Kozyrev et al., "Critical Ignoring as a Core Competence for Digital Citizens" (ASSOCIATION FOR PSYCHOLOGICAL SCIENCE, 2023).

She offers the perfect social media scenario we go through daily:

You sit down to think about how you'll pay for next month's bills or what you'll buy your mate for Valentine's Day. Great! That sounds productive… but wait! A headline catches your attention:

"They thought it was a spy balloon, but when the defense department shot it down, they were SHOCKED to see this inside."

You click on the link, and the next thing you know, it's lunchtime. *Wait, how did that happen*, you ask yourself?

In the last chapter, we learned that we have very little defense against clickbait, thanks to our prefrontal cortex. Its primary job is finding unique things for our brain, so when you see that latest Bigfoot story or the "Top 5 Air Fryer recipes to solve dinner problems forever," you go there.

So, how do we fight this madness? Let's get to the core of what Dr. Boardman found:

"Critical ignoring — deliberately and strategically choosing what to disregard and where to invest one's limited attentional capacities — is an essential life skill for citizens of the digital world. In addition to keeping us informed, critical ignoring can also help us stay sane."

I became intrigued by these tips because they not only enhance your personal life but also serve as effective tools in combating misinformation, a key component in the recipe for uprisings.

Dr. Boardman's top tips to strengthen our battle shields in the online war for our attention include:

Tip #1:
Self-Nudging

As we saw earlier, low-quality headlines are as tempting to our prefrontal cortex as snacks are to our eager taste buds. Dr. Boardman states you shouldn't blame yourself, though. They want what they want. After all, who can resist that tiramisu you see in the desert case?

How many of you have lowered your cravings at home for Ben and Jerry's Rocky Road by simply not having it around? This hack works pretty darn well – if it's out of reach, you simply can't have it. You haven't stopped the cravings forever; you've just limited your reach.

The same thing works for social media – eliminating the most distracting apps will help you regain some of that time. Can I offer a personal challenge and success story?

Like you, I struggle with those headlines about Bigfoot and Spy Balloons. I have ADHD, so perhaps it's another layer of defense I don't have.

I took Dr. Boardman's advice and examined my social media usage for two weeks. I documented the time I spent on each app and noted whenever a headline or comment elicited a negative reaction from me. Based on what you know, which social media app do you think was my downfall?

I couldn't blame you if you guessed Instagram or Facebook, but my weakness was Twitter. I continually found myself heading down a rabbit hole reading other people's tweets to the tune of about 1.5 hours per week. But why Twitter?

There may be a scientific reason for my increased reactions on Twitter. Twitter is different enough to make a big difference in viewing its content.

Twitter limits your tweets to only 4,000 characters (if you're a paid subscriber), so the tweets you read, especially from politicians, are designed to be noticed without much "fluff." By design, they must grab or lose our attention (and believe me, they want it). Do politicians understand this attention-grabbing secret? Absolutely.

According to a study of 3 million Facebook and Twitter posts from US media and politicians by the University of Cambridge, "slamming political rivals may be the most effective way to go viral – revealing social media's perverse incentives.[83]"

Consider these clickbaitable headlines from some of our Senators and Political Influencers:

"Do your wife and father-in-law know about your girlfriends? I wonder if she'll remain faithful when you're in prison". Yikes, and yes, that's a real tweet from a US Senator.

And who can forget this gem read live to millions of viewers from a major cable news anchor: "That is the President of the United States. That is the most powerful person in the world, and we see him like an obese turtle on his back flailing in the hot sun."

So, I decided to plan my break-up with Twitter. Like any difficult break-up, it wasn't easy, yet I knew the relationship had turned toxic. Long story short, I felt better after severing this relationship. I'm equally happy to say that I save about 1.25 hours per week by breaking up with Twitter. I call that a win.

Now, don't get me wrong, I still use social media. In fact, some of the content from this book was referenced from sites like Facebook and

---

[83] Fred Lewsey, "Slamming Political Rivals May Be the Most Effective Way to Go viralFred Lewsey," University of Cambridge, June 22, 2021, https://www.cam.ac.uk/stories/viralpolitics.

other political sites. I didn't use Twitter for any reason except to find sensational headlines for this book. 😊

Which social media platform is your time vacuum?

Tip #2:
Adopt a *Do Not Feed the Trolls* Attitude

How many times have you responded to a friend's Facebook message claiming something that you know is incredibly false? Like a post from your friend's feed claiming a secret cabal of pet detectives hired by the city is coming for her dog because she hasn't paid her yearly pet license fee.

Sure, you may offer some online leniency because she's your friend. Yet what about those times you've responded to someone you don't even know? It could be over an issue you really care about, like gun rights, climate change, or those secret spy balloons.

Let me ask a serious question though: How many times have you changed someone's mind about an issue online as a direct result of your tweet or post? You already know the answer. It's the same as how many people fall for that robocall warning you that your car warranty may be expired: 0, null, zip.

Tip #3:
If You Really Want Unbiased News, Seek Unbiased News Stations

I mentioned in an earlier chapter that most people overwhelmingly want to hear both sides of a large issue in their news feed. But is this enough to make people switch news sources?

Before you cease watching CNN or Fox News in your quest for more balanced news, know that there are plenty of other reasons for breaking up with these news stations. First and foremost, that harmful, unnoticeable adrenaline rush you get (aka...." trigger impulse") will decrease. That alone should make it worthwhile, yet here are a few more benefits of watching less biased news:

- Watching more balanced news enhances your capacity to consider diverse viewpoints and fosters greater understanding towards others.
- You may connect with more people who want realistic changes in our government and world.

Now, some *good* news: There are many sources out there to help you switch. One of those sources that helps you find less biased news is the site allsides.com. It features a user-friendly graphical interface that assesses the bias of news sources and highlights platforms with lower bias ratings.

Is it possible to find 100% unbiased news?

Unfortunately, even with the best intentions, this isn't possible, nor should we expect it. This is primarily due to our personal psychological enemy, confirmation bias. Nevertheless, I can personally vouch for the numerous psychological benefits you'll experience by making this transition and discovering a new platform that more equitably assesses both sides of the political spectrum.

Tip #4:

Hit Social Media and Biased News Stations Where it Counts – In Their Pocketbook

You've already read that spreading misinformation and sewing nuggets of hate is big business for news sources. It's a simple equation - the louder the megaphone, the more media companies financially gain.

But would you support an internet platform that made it okay to spread international terrorism? The family of Nohemi Gonzales presents a compelling case on how Google's YouTube did just that.

Nohemi Gonzales was a student who was visiting Paris in the fall of 2015. That week should have been a memorable week for her. She was experiencing the sights and sounds of Paris, taking in the city, and enjoying the company of friends at local bistros and other locations.

On November 13th, 2015, multiple ISIS members carried out coordinated attacks that killed 130 people throughout the city. Nohemi was among those whose life was cut short. Unfortunately, she was simply at the wrong place at the wrong time, and this fateful timing led to her death.[84]

The Islamic State would claim responsibility for the attack.

Her family was outraged to learn that the Islamic State was allowed to recruit and radicalize new members on the YouTube platform prior to her death.

After this horrific attack, a law firm specializing in suing companies that aid terrorists reached out to Nohemi's family to assist in filing a lawsuit against the internet giant.

The suit claimed Google's YouTube contributed to her death by knowingly allowing ISIS members to recruit and radicalize members who eventually coordinated this horrific attack. By allowing this content, lawyers for the parents claim YouTube broke the U.S. Antiterrorism Act by promoting Islamic propaganda videos through its algorithms.

---

[84] Barbara E. Murphy, "Remembering Nohemi Gonzalez, a Year Later," The New York Times, November 4, 2016, https://www.nytimes.com/2016/11/06/education/edlife/remembering-nohemi-gonzalez-a-year-later.html.

A Google spokesperson offered an empty condolence, "Our hearts go out to the victims of terrorism and their families everywhere... YouTube has a strong track record of taking swift action against terrorist content. We have clear policies prohibiting terrorist recruitment and content intending to incite violence and quickly remove videos violating these policies when flagged by our users.[85]"

But was this statement true? Did their policy go far enough to stop terrorists from utilizing their platform?

At the heart of Nohemi's parents' case is the responsibility YouTube had concerning its algorithm. They contend YouTube knew that their algorithm would promote any content (including terrorist content) and did little to stop it.

Most people would agree that it is difficult for a content provider like YouTube to review every piece of content on their site. Yet one of the powers the video giant YouTube and other large social media platforms have is governance over their algorithms and the ability to better flag propaganda, terrorist recruitment messages, and other dangerous traffic.

You shouldn't be allowed to type in "Islamic State" videos and be fed a diet of videos that contain terrorist recruitment messages. Yet her family's lawyers state that's exactly what YouTube allowed to happen.

Here's another twist: YouTube did not dispute that they allowed their algorithms to present terrorist content, but instead of limiting liability, their primary defense was leveraging section 230 of the Communications Decency Act of 1996, which shields internet companies from liability.

---

[85] Alex Johnson and Raul A Reyes, "Father of American Killed in Paris Attacks Sues Twitter, Facebook, Google," NBCNews.com, June 16, 2016, https://www.nbcnews.com/storyline/paris-terror-attacks/family-american-killed-paris-attacks-sues-twitter-facebook-google-n593351.

The case received a lot of attention and was heard at the Supreme Court. On May 18, 2023, the Supreme Court sided with Google, Twitter, and Facebook in lawsuits, holding them not liable for terrorist attacks.[86]

This case directly parallels domestic terrorists' use of Facebook during the January 6th insurrection, a full 5 years after the Nohemi case, in which Facebook knowingly allowed dangerous content on their sites.

You read earlier how Facebook shirked some of its accountability, which partly allowed the insurrectionists to storm the Capitol on January 6th. There's no denying this occurred. Multiple insurrectionists used Facebook to organize and communicate their plans for the 'Stop the Steal' movement.[87]

Like the YouTube case above, much of Facebook whistleblower data scientist Frances Haugen's testimony to Congress focused on the belief that Facebook "chose to maximize its growth rather than implement safeguards on its platforms." She went on to state, "The result has been more division, more harm, more lies…and in some cases, this dangerous online talk has led to actual violence that harms and kills people.[88]"

86 "Supreme Court Avoids Ruling on Law Shielding Social Media Companies," Spectrum News NY 1, May 18, 2023, https://ny1.com/nyc/all-boroughs/politics/2023/05/18/supreme-court-avoids-ruling-on-law-shielding-social-media-companies.

87 Craig Silverman et al., "Facebook Hosted Surge of Misinformation and Insurrection Threats in Months Leading up to Jan. 6 Attack, Records Show," ProPublica, January 4, 2022, https://www.propublica.org/article/facebook-hosted-surge-of-misinformation-and-insurrection-threats-in-months-leading-up-to-jan-6-attack-records-show.

88 Bobby Allyn, "Here Are 4 Key Points from the Facebook Whistleblower's Testimony on Capitol Hill," NPR, October 6, 2021, https://www.npr.org/2021/10/05/1043377310/facebook-whistleblower-frances-haugen-congress.

Should companies like YouTube be held liable when their algorithms recommend terrorist content?

Politicians don't agree on much, yet there is bi-partisan legislation designed to shed light on what social media does with all the information they collect and hold them accountable to take meaningful action.[89] Before you say it's not their job, please remember both Google and Facebook make billions of dollars per year and are currently fully protected from harm by section 230 of the Communications Decency Act.[90] Improving their algorithms shouldn't be an expense another family should have to pay for with their son or daughter's life.

If this angers you, if you feel internet companies can do a better job at content moderation, write, or contact your State Senator to support the Platform Accountability and Transparency Act on the official government site.[91]

Let's move on to another source that has done irreparable harm in dividing us...cable news, and public enemy #1 of our increased polarization.

You just learned how Big Tech has used an outdated law created in 1996 to shirk its responsibility for better managing dangerous content.

---

89 Cory Combs, "Council for Responsible Social Media Endorses Bipartisan Platform Accountability and Transparency Act," Issue One, July 6, 2023, https://issueone.org/press/council-for-responsible-social-media-endorses-bipartisan-platform-accountability-and-transparency-act/.

90 Barbara Ortutay, "What You Should Know about Section 230, the Rule That Shaped Today's Internet," PBS, February 21, 2023, https://www.pbs.org/newshour/politics/what-you-should-know-about-section-230-the-rule-that-shaped-todays-internet#:~:text=That's%20thanks%20to%20Section%20230,by%20another%20information%20content%20provider.%E2%80%9D.

91 Contact your state senator here: https://www.senate.gov/general/contacting

But what about the two big cable networks that promote misinformation, division, and biased news stations? It turns out they cleverly hide behind an outdated law as well.

Here's why that matters: If we're going to slow down our war of misinformation, feeling of divide, and some type of uprising, we must make them more accountable.

Before I present the next misinformation heavyweights, here's a statistic: a 2021 Reuters poll stated that 74% of respondents want news outlets "to reflect a range of different views and leave it to them to decide.[92]"

Does this sound like you? If so, then welcome to the majority. Most of us (except that Uncle of yours on Thanksgiving, who knows all) really want to hear the 'whole story', multiple angles from a story, and then be able to make up our minds after hearing various sides of an issue.

The problem isn't what we want. The problem is what we're getting from the major social networks and news platforms.

So, what's going wrong?

When most people claim, "our country has never been more divided", they struggle to identify the source of this division. However, you'll see that according to researchers who study causes of polarization, public enemy number one for our divisions is the relentless 24-hour propaganda machines (with a little news thrown in) in the United States, CNN, and Fox.

---

[92] Dr Craig T. Robertson, "Impartiality Unpacked: A Study of Four Countries," Reuters Institute for the Study of Journalism, June 23, 2021, https://reutersinstitute.politics.ox.ac.uk/digital-news-report/2021/impartiality-unpacked-study-four-countries.

For some, CNN is the enemy if you lean right, and Fox News is the enemy if you lean left. You shouldn't feel bad about this. It's instinctual to seek sources that validate our perspective and to feel a sense of belonging with those who share our views.

Again, no judging, regardless of which station you favor. But let's dig deeper to see how this may be harming your objectivity.

Do CNN and Fox News report real events? Sure. Do they have a political tilt? Absolutely. Even more crucially, we should be asking whether their deliberate production of biased news fosters division among us.

It's a neurological fact that constant exposure to messages that confirm what you're observing can eventually lead certain individuals to believe that this reflects reality - and that presents a huge safety issue for our country as we discovered on January 6th, 2021.

The science of which network you favor is not by accident.

According to an online article in Science, maximizing online engagement leads to increased polarization. The co-authors of an article titled 'How Tech Platforms Fuel U.S. Polarization and What Government Can Do About It" write this is "in part because of the contagious power of content that elicits sectarian fear.[93]"

It's easy to verify how accurate this is by just sampling the people you've unfriended on Facebook due to their extremely polarized posts. Were they always this way?

All of this polarization can't be attributed to social media. Yet researchers found in a March 2020 study that subjects who stayed

[93] (Barrett et al., 2023)

off Facebook for a month "significantly reduced polarization of views on policy issues.[94]"

Both cable stations have been guilty of putting the other "side" into negative camps.

Check out these headlines meant to cater to the network's core viewers, then rate them as *fair* or *biased.*

The first is from a CNN headline that appeared after two Senators interrupted President Biden's 2023 State of the Union Speech:

"Republicans' extreme reaction to Biden's big speech helps make his point."

This may seem like an innocent headline to you if you're a Democrat, but it doesn't *feel* innocent if you're a Republican. It feels like you're attacking the entire Republican base. Please note I'm not condoning interrupting the President, but a more accurate headline could have read "Two Republicans Interrupt President Biden's 2023 State of the Union Speech". There. It's accurate without showing political bias.

Let's dig deep into our biased tendencies to find out why.

First, using words like "extreme" to describe *whole groups of people* incites tribalism (remember, only 2 of 52 Republican Senators interrupted President Biden's 2023 State of the Union Speech). It's also politically slanted ("...extreme reaction to Biden's big speech helps make his point"). According to whom? Supposedly, this is an impartial news network making these claims.

---

[94] Hunt Allcott et al., "The Welfare Effects of Social Media," American Economic Review, March 2020, https://www.aeaweb.org/articles?id=10.1257%2Faer.20190658.

This type of reporting does exactly what the company owners want… to incite anger and score points with the base of people who favor CNN.

Fox News also plays this same game: "Biden knows his student loan handout is such a loser, he wouldn't even talk about it." Yikes, where do I start other than to say it's incredibly politically loaded and lands exactly where it was supposed to land… in toxic territory.

Given this data, we have to wonder why news stations try so hard to foster animosity toward the other side.

The answer may be pure greed. I'm sure you've heard the adage "follow the money." In 2020, Fox News raked in $1.8 billion, followed by CNN's $714 million cash haul.[95] They are literally being paid to divide us.

But just how does a political problem and polarization lead to an uprising?

We've seen from previous civil wars that a political problem can become a *humanity* problem. People begin to feel hopeless about resolving issues peacefully and turn to conflict instead.

In the Yugoslav Wars from 1991 to 2001 and in the conflict in Northern Ireland from the 1960s to 1998, this division eventually led to neighbor against neighbor.

Other analysts besides myself who study civil war are also concerned. "America is a special country, but when you study the hundreds of civil wars that have broken out since World War II, as I have, you come to understand that we are not immune to conflict. Here, too,

---

[95] "Total Profit for Cable TV (Fox News, CNN and MSNBC)," Pew Research Center's Journalism Project, June 7, 2023, https://www.pewresearch.org/journalism/chart/sotnm-cable-total-profit-for-cable-tv/.

we fight for political power to protect a way of life. Here, too, we buy guns when we feel threatened. So, in those moments when I would prefer to look away or take comfort in the voice that says, no, that could never happen here, I think of all that political science has taught me. I think about the facts before us.[96]"

It's time to fight back.

Ezra Klein, a New York Times journalist, puts it best in his article "It's time for media to choose: Neutrality or Democracy." It seems ironic that you have a journalist making this statement, but the truth of the matter is journalists are just like you and I, and many see their publications turning into garbage dumps.

As mentioned earlier, 74% of us want news that presents views from the other side, in essence, "fair and balanced" news, yet that same poll found only 29% of people trust news "most of the time.[97]" (By the way, who are the other 26% that want biased news??) Instead of looking at all the reasons why the media is broke, why not seek innovative solutions that improve it?

One group called *Spectacles* offers a common-sense solution by doing just that.

To do that, we're going across the pond to three countries that enjoy both high marks for their public media and high trust in their news sources.

Citizens in Finland, Portugal, and Kenya rate their trust level of news as 57% or higher. That may not seem ground-breaking, but it's 100%

---

96 (Walter, 2023)

97 "21 Findings from the Reuters Institute's Research in 2021 Still Relevant in 2022," Reuters Institute for the Study of Journalism, December 21, 2021, https://reutersinstitute.politics.ox.ac.uk/news/21-findings-reuters-institutes-research-2021-still-relevant-2022.

higher than the answer Americans provided when asked to rate their trustworthiness of news.[98]

Spectacles dissected these variables and found one common element in these countries: a hybrid model of news that brings together a private-media style of news coupled with public-medias' programming free of negative incentives, which is often the driver behind the biased message you see.

I know what you're saying. Isn't our American public media NPR? The answer is no.

Our public news is called the Corporation for Public Broadcasting (CPB), and it's a private corporation funded by the American people. NPR only receives 5% of this budget, while 80% goes to local television.

Is the CPB's news content as commercial, flashy, and marketed as CNN and Fox News? I'll leave that up to you. Yet, if you're currently reading this and usually don't watch local news content created by the CPB, you already know the answer.

Yet don't blame it on the hard-working staff at this agency. Blame it on funding. Our country's leaders seem to have little appetite to feed more money into this important endeavor.

It's too bad because there is a direct correlation between funding and receiving higher quality, less biased news. In fact, Public Media funding in Norway and Sweden ranges from $85 to nearly $125 per capita, while their citizen's trust in media reaches levels of 57% and above.

---

[98] Amy Watson, "Trust in News Media Worldwide 2023," Statista, June 14, 2023, https://www.statista.com/statistics/308468/importance-brand-journalist-creating-trust-news/.

Compare that to the United States, which spends a dismal $1.40 per capita to fund public media.[99]

I would argue we could find other ways to cut the budget and increase the effectiveness of our public news, which may bring our polarization a notch or two. For example, the US taxpayers spent $560,000 to study the effects of fish on treadmills and $450,000 to determine if dinosaurs could sing.[100] (For the record, it was determined dinosaurs did not have the vocal structure to sing – so don't anticipate their presence on The Voice if dinosaurs ever return.)

As the organization Spectacles writes in their video titled "Public Media Does Not Equal Propaganda" on YouTube, "without sufficient funding, the CPB model stands no chance against the tide of sensationalism and the behemoth of cable news.[101]"

Having stronger public media isn't a miracle drug that will fix our divide issues but considering that our current news giants are a large reason for our polarization, it doesn't mean we shouldn't fund them more.

There's one more worrisome correlation between public media funding and the fate of our democracy: those democratic countries with the highest rating on the "The Democracy Index" also enjoyed more creative and enjoyable public media.

---

[99] Victor Pickard and Timothy Neff, "Op-Ed: Strengthen Our Democracy by Funding Public Media," Columbia Journalism Review, June 2, 2021, https://www.cjr.org/opinion/public-funding-media-democracy.php.

[100] Andrew Lisa, "32 Wildest Things Your Taxes Are Paying For," GOBankingRates, May 24, 2023, https://www.gobankingrates.com/taxes/tax-laws/shocking-things-taxes-pay-for/.

[101] "[Vid] Why Public Media Isn't Propaganda (but Sometimes Is)," Spectacles Media, May 12, 2023, https://www.spectacles.news/public-media-and-propaganda/#fn1.

The Democracy Index measures those elements considered benchmarks of democracy, such as fair and free elections, civil liberties, and how its citizens perceive corruption in their government.[102]

Countries with higher scores have very little chance of having an uprising, while countries with lower scores are vulnerable to civil unrest. Unfortunately, the United States has been backsliding since 2012.[103]

I've offered a lot of routes on how you can make a difference in making better media choices and how you can fight back against media sources who are determined to divide us. Listed below is a summary of these routes to help you act:

1. Forget critical thinking when it comes to social media – work on honing your skills in critical ignoring.
2. Break up with the apps that generate the most negative reactions from you.
3. Replace your biased news with sources that favor giving you both sides of an issue. Head to allsides.com or Google other media evaluation sites for other sources.
4. Consider adding your name to the Platform Accountability and Transparency Act to ensure social media companies are sharing their data to improve the effects platforms have on our lives – it's one of the few bipartisan pieces of legislation that both political sides agree on.

---

[102] "Most Democratic Countries 2023," Wisevoter, May 2, 2023, https://wisevoter.com/country-rankings/most-democratic-countries/.

[103] Anna Fleck and Felix Richter, "Infographic: The State of Democracy in the U.S.," Statista Daily Data, July 4, 2022, https://www.statista.com/chart/27719/united-states-democracy-index/.

You've read enough of politicians, social media, and our network news behaving badly.

Up next, we're going to work on you – we'll explore the reason why you might be experiencing a shorter fuse lately when it comes to others and, most importantly, what you can do to alleviate these triggers.

Chapter 8

Help!
My Amygdala's Been Hijacked!

Have you ever encountered a moment when someone's words or actions provoked such intense anger that you found it difficult to control your response? In this out-of-control moment you may have thrown things like an NFL quarterback and used some words that you didn't even know were in your personal dictionary. The aftermath may have left you feeling miserable.

Even today, it may still remain a mystery to you why the event transpired and why you couldn't prevent yourself from engaging in these actions.

Today you'll learn the science that explains why these occurrences occur, explore how the pandemic and political stress may be triggering even more similar events, and most importantly, strategies to redirect these sometimes life-changing anger bombs in the future.

Let's look at a real-life scenario below (the names have been changed to protect the innocent).

Julie let out a weary sigh while she watched the recent barrage of negative news in the airport lobby, anticipating her flight. Yet another school shooting occurred. An apartment fire in a low-income neighborhood left several residents stranded, and she caught the tail end of a story about a biker who was killed by a hit-and-run driver, leaving a wife and 3 children fatherless.

Politicians were still fighting about the nation's southern border, and on top of that, the Supreme Court overturned Roe Vs. Wade, an issue that she felt passionate about. Julie understood the other side's opinion, but the Supreme Court decision did not sit well with her.

Often known as a positive person with a high emotional IQ, Julie had started to feel the toll of the daily stream of negative world events. The mounting sense of anger and frustration in the world that didn't align with her values was about to manifest in an unexpected manner.

Julie knew just what to do to help her feel better.

When times get tough, Julie has a magical circle of friends who never fail to lift her spirits. She'd known these friends for years, and they always seemed to clear away the dark clouds that appeared periodically in her life. Her friends were her sanctuary and a needed prescription for forgetting about those world events she had grown accustomed to seeing on her news app.

Before boarding her flight, Julie sent a group text to her circle of girlfriends, pleading for a night out. Soon after the text, she received 5 responses from friends who would join her.

The night was set! The thought of getting together with her trusted tribe of friends put a much-needed smile on her face. She suggested meeting at a trendy new restaurant that had just opened nearby.

The night began innocently enough. They covered the latest news with each other which included updates on one friend's engagement and planned details for the exciting return of *Girl's Weekend* in Vegas that COVID-19 had sidelined the previous two years.

Wine flowed freely, laughter abounded, and the night was off to a splendid start.

One of Julie's friends brought another friend named Marie, whom Julie had never met. Marie didn't speak much, but her strong opinions on world events were quite evident. Julie was okay with that. In fact, the more friends, the merrier she thought.

Yet as the night continued, she could feel herself becoming increasingly annoyed by Marie. She thought to herself, *Why would someone voice such strong opinions in a group of people she doesn't even know?*

The wine helped soothe Julie's ruffled feathers. Plus, it was such a relief to be with her friends and reminisce about the past.

After about an hour, Marie brought up the subject of the Supreme Court's decision to overturn Roe v. Wade. Marie didn't offer a controversial opinion. She merely mentioned that the decision would drastically change the status quo. Most of the group treaded lightly on the subject, and some said nothing at all, for fear of an argument or worse.

Julie couldn't quite catch what Marie was saying, yet judging from body language, she inferred that Marie held opposing views on a woman's right to choose.

Without warning, some type of trigger was activated within Julie. Incensed, she stood up and faced Marie. "How dare you come in here and drop your "pro-life" opinion on us! You have no idea what other women have gone through," she yelled. "Aren't you sick and tired of men making decisions about our bodies?" She scolded Marie, stating that "if she knew what was good for her, she'd stick up for women in the next election."

A fun night out had suddenly turned confrontational and uncomfortable. The outburst only lasted a few seconds. After Julie's outburst, the group sat stunned, including Marie, who was searching for the nearest exit.

The reason for Julie's reaction can be attributed to a phenomenon known as the "Amygdala Hijack", a term coined by author and neuropsychologist Daniel Goleman.

Have you ever had a similar reaction in which you felt out of control?

Of course, most of us have.

If you've recently become more agitated and less forgiving than in the past, you're not alone. Psychologists say in today's hyper-confrontational political world, these types of hijacks are on the rise.

According to the American Psychological Association, "the COVID-19 pandemic, racial injustice, and political divisiveness…shows a battered American psyche, facing a barrage of external stressors that are mostly out of personal control.[104]"

So why are we talking about it? What does it have to do with preventing uprisings?

Recall in Chapter Two that all uprisings contain emotional and political reasons for occurring. So one way to battle against sustained political confrontation is to heal our nation…from the inside out. The more tools we have to face this brave new world, the better we'll be able to lower our nation's conflict barometer.

There are additional benefits for learning how to better handle conflict.

104 "Stress in America 2022: Concerned for the Future, Beset by Inflation," American Psychological Association, October 2022, https://www.apa.org/news/press/releases/stress/2022/concerned-future-inflation.

I've led many conflict management classes, and I can testify that learning your conflict style and identifying the warning signs prior to a hijack occurring will improve your personal relationships.

Several participants have contacted me weeks after a class, sharing that they were able to persuade their partners to seek professional counseling after learning some of these techniques, or contacted a counselor for themselves.

Learning how to better handle conflicts can not only save a relationship but help put antiseptic on our country's open wounds.

Please note something important. Your first reaction when you disagree with someone is usually not patience or understanding. I get that.

Learning better self-regulation and conflict management is not about agreeing with another person's view of the world. Author Priscilla Shirer offers that "oneness" is understanding that others' personal opinions may be different from yours.[105]

So, let's learn a little more about this funny thing called the Amygdala Hijack that produces a not-so-funny overreaction.

Understand that the amygdala is not the enemy. Its purpose is to create a quick response to a perceived threat. This threat doesn't have to be a situation like running when you see a tiger that escaped from a zoo. The danger your amygdala feels can be as simple as someone you perceive who's attacking your morals, family name, or other values you deem important.

Here's what's going on in our brain before and during the hijack.

---

[105] See more of Priscilla Shirer's wisdom on this page: https://quotlr.com/author/priscilla-shirer#google_vignette

First, an external stimulus appears that sets off alarm bells as our brains attempt to process an unknown person or idea. Remember when Julie encountered the unfamiliar Marie on her night out with friends? Julie's amygdala was working to determine the proper response when faced with Marie's perceived threat to her values.

Now, here's the difficult part to understand: Neuroscientists believe that as much as 80% of the time you can control your response to a negative attack, for example, if someone personally insulted you at a party. Woohoo! Thank our good friend evolution for that.

It's the remaining 20% that remains a mystery which may cause this downward spiral we witnessed with Julie.

When that 20% appears, our amygdala goes into fast, uncontrolled motion. In less than 1/8th of a second, blood drains from our brain, and we lose 75% of our ability to think clearly. According to neuroscientists, your poor neocortex is unable to help you now. The amygdala is in full hijack as it races to protect us from the real or perceived threat.

During this hijack, intense emotions surface, as they did with Julie, and we find ourselves unable to govern our subsequent thoughts. Our heart rate soars and our palms sweat as adrenaline rushes through our bodies. Some have stated they experienced goosebumps on their skin during the event.

This uncontrolled response usually seems like forever for the individual going through it. In reality, the physical effects last about 18 minutes.

Whew! I'm glad this explanation is over. Yet the worst may not be over for Julie and others who experience the hijack. They will most likely experience a hangover of feelings ranging from guilt to fear.

To help my students understand how to combat these issues better, we first help them learn to be aware of which life circumstances may trigger this hijack.

A hijack can manifest for many reasons, but the loss of a loved one, extreme fatigue, a severe health issue, along with the added stress of current events, like COVID-19, can render you more vulnerable to experiencing one.

Let's revisit Julie's hijack event. When put under the microscope, numerous factors could have contributed to this occurrence.

Her mother had recently been diagnosed with Hodgkin's disease. Her mother's declining health placed an emotional toll on both Julie and her family. Julie knew her mother had missed several doctor's appointments due to the COVID-19 lockdown. Meaning her diagnosis and treatment were delayed, possibly worsening her condition.

Julie was also highly sensitive to a recent social issue that pushed on her sense of civil liberties. You are more inclined to perceive a personal attack from someone you don't know if you sense that they are being disrespectful to you, and this trigger set the stage for Marie, who unfortunately was at the wrong place at the wrong time.

But was Julie's reaction avoidable? Are we immune to this overreaction that occurs in times of high stress?

The good news is neuroscientists have some strategies that may help.

Let's look at 4 constructive ways to battle back to sanity.

Tip #1:

Understand Your Limits During Times of High Personal Stress

If you've had a recent relationship break, experienced the death of a loved one, or had a personal health issue, understand that you are already prone to these unexpected outbursts.

Psychologists highly recommend taking additional time for self-care if you're feeling overwhelmed during these high-stress times in your life.

It's easy to believe that you can manage all the stress, but the toll it takes on your mind and body can leave you feeling utterly burnt out. You can't take care of others if you can't take care of yourself.

Commit to spending time for yourself, whatever that looks like.

Tip #2:
Be Vulnerable – Confide in Someone About Your Anger

First, it's okay to be vulnerable after an event occurs (yes, I'm looking at you, men of the earth). Studies show that men and women lose their temper fairly equally, but men express their anger more outwardly, and this inability to channel some of this anger can get them into trouble.[106]

When I say "be vulnerable," I mean just that. It's socially acceptable for men to vent their anger to friends, but they seldom express their inability to control their rage. Even during times of high duress, like losing a friend, we won't usually confide in a friend about this issue.

Avoidance is not a healthy way to march through life, and not discussing these feelings can return to haunt us. Talking to someone, even if it's not a close friend, may allow your feelings to dissipate, giving you time to reflect instead of experiencing the exploding volcano effect.

While reading this, I know some of you may still hesitate to ask others for help. Think about this: Would you think differently about

---

[106] Ryan Martin, "Are Men Angrier than Women?," Psychology Today, June 21, 2021, https://www.psychologytoday.com/us/blog/all-the-rage/202106/are-men-angrier-women.

a friend who confided in you that they were experiencing unusually higher amounts of anger or bouts of rage during times of grief or personal loss? Of course not, you'd want to help them.

So, confide in them - for yourself and others.

Tip #3:
Learn to Reroute a Hijack Before It Occurs

If triggered, we have less than .08 of a second to react before experiencing one of these hijacks. That's not a lot of time, yet in my workshops, I've discovered that re-creating a scenario that previously caused you grief in the past can be instrumental in preventing its recurrence. I call this 'pre-exposure' therapy because it involves mentally reimagining a difficult event from the past, and then substituting a different scenario for how it could play out. This can re-route that potential anger before it arrives.

I've included a useful worksheet for self-study (courtesy of Dr. Lori Wieters) on my website, but we'll also go through the exercise here.

Building Awareness Exercise

Think about a real situation that caused an emotional hijack to appear. What happened? Write down what you believe the trigger(s) were and what emotions you felt.

When________________________ happened, I felt __________________ (use one of the core emotional responses – mad, sad, glad, or scared to describe your emotion)

Did the hijack appear in proximity to a personal event (death, birth, significant health issue, holiday, relation breakup, stressful work situation, etc.?) ____

What personal value was being compromised or violated? ________
____

Now let's diagram a better response if it reappears again:

In that same situation, what other choices do you wish you had made?

____

____

How would the results have changed?

____

What action will you take next time?

____

Take a couple of minutes and replay the new situation in your mind.

Do not stay in this space now that you've recreated this event. There's no reason to dwell on it. Instead, give yourself credit for taking the time to improve your well-being.

Also, remember the other strategies we discussed here to further improve your ability to control that response. (Just a reminder to print this worksheet on our website and complete it.)

Tip #4:
The Thomas Jefferson Brain Hack

Thomas Jefferson, founding father of the United States, framer of the Declaration of Independence, 3rd President of the United States, and therapist.

Wait, what? Therapist?

Well, not officially, yet his advice on controlling anger is still valid today.

We are emotional beings, and controlling our emotions is sometimes difficult. As you discovered, we don't have a long time to react to overpowering emotions which sometimes occur. It's an automatic response. But are we powerless against these negative hijacks?

Absolutely not! But it takes exposure therapy to improve our reaction.

Our brain has a hack that most of us don't know about, except perhaps Thomas Jefferson, who said, "When angry, count to 10 before you speak. If very angry, a hundred".

So counting to 10 can actually prevent us from overreacting?

Yes, and here's the biological explanation.

As you engage in counting, the frontal lobe becomes active, and this distraction may allow just enough time for the prefrontal cortex to calm down or escape the situation.

So the next time you get angry, try counting to 10 or using a similar easy math problem. I like multiplying 2x2 and continuing to multiply the result by 2 again. What equation you use to count isn't critical. What truly matters is the neurological processes taking place in your brain as you process this information.

Try it the next time you're stuck in traffic or when you get annoyed behind one of those drivers who forgot that the left lane is a passing lane.

That was a significant amount of self-therapy. For many, these tools to reprogram uncontrolled responses mark the start of enhanced relationships and a renewed confidence in effectively managing emotions. So how do you feel?

Here's a quick summary:

- Economic stress, political divisiveness, social injustices, and the lingering effects of COVID have left most of us feeling overly anxious. These factors have contributed to a rise in conflicts and a decline in personal well-being.
- Increasing self-care can help decrease stress caused by these events.
- Talking to someone about uncontrollable anger is not socially acceptable. Asking for help from friends and close relationships can assist with finding alternatives to anger.
- Learning to reroute a hijack before it appears can help you diagram a better response for future events and leads to improved relationships and careers.

If this chapter hits home and you'd like to better understand hijacks and how to avoid them, please sign up for our Masterclass on our linktree or website http://coachingforevolution.com.

Important Note: I hope these tips help you better handle your emotions during stressful times. Yet, this advice is no substitute for professional counseling with a licensed therapist. A professional counselor is there to help. Consider how different your life and other lives could be with consistent, effective assistance.

In this chapter, we've learned to re-route our emotions if they get hijacked, but how do we learn to get along with those whose politics differ vastly from ours?

In the section ahead, I also wanted to share my personal, sometimes emotionally painful struggle, with a father whom I didn't see eye to eye politically with. Some of the methods I've listed in the following chapter allowed us to find our way home and forge a strong bond together before he passed away.

We need all the love and care we can get in today's world, and I hope my story allows you to mend broken fences, even in difficult times.

We're going to tackle that in our next chapter. Coming Up: MAGA Hats and Snowflakes: Who Do You See America?

Chapter 9

MAGA Hats and Snowflakes: Who Do You See America?

When you see a person walking down the street wearing a red 'Make America Great Again' hat, who do you see?

Do you feel a connection with the person or do your thoughts about the person race somewhere else in your mind? Unless you know them, it may be impossible to also see this person as someone who overcame polio as a child and had to deal with the loss of his wife after she was killed suddenly in a car accident. If you got to know him, could you envision this same man as a wonderful father to 4 children whom he adopted? (I have a secret about this man that I'll share later.)

What's your first reaction when you view a person wearing a "Black Lives Matter" shirt?

Irrespective of your personal stance on the Black Lives Matter movement, did you judge the individual's entire identity solely based on her shirt? If you get to know her, you may have discovered that she's a proud parent to a first-generation college graduate and gathers enough strength to volunteer weekly at a food bank despite a recent Parkinson's diagnosis. Your opinion of her may also be altered after learning she recently attended the funerals of two nephews who died from indiscriminate gun violence.

As humans, we evolved to quickly assess someone as a friend or foe. This helps bring order to our world. Yet, in the previous chapter, you've also read that the media you watch profoundly affects your social lens and influences you to believe something about that person they are not.

When you pass judgment on the individual, our lens often fails to provide a comprehensive understanding of that person, shaped by our family upbringing and other influential factors. This inability to offer a nuanced perception of the complete person can prove a dangerous flaw in some people.

In reality, we are a paradox of different personal characteristics.

We're going to learn about *dialectical thinking* to help us examine and reconcile opposing perspectives of someone you may have cut out of your life due to political differences or another long-standing disagreement.

Dialectical thinking creates space for evaluating the whole person so we can let go of the anger, resentment, and frustration we feel toward the individual. It will also help you understand why we need to consider the person's entire personality instead of just a hat or shirt.

The person I'll use as a perfect paradox of positive and negative traits is my stepfather, who you may have guessed was the individual I was writing about in the chapter's opening.

My stepfather grew up in a family in the 1940s in Omaha, Nebraska, a Midwestern city near the Missouri River. Nebraska has deep agricultural roots and is the headquarters of many Fortune 500 companies like Berkshire Hathaway. This state is proud of its football team, which, unfortunately, has been in a "rebuilding year" for the last 20 years.

My stepfather grew up in a predominantly white neighborhood. His father often used racist words to describe black people. My stepfather learned it was culturally acceptable for him and his friends to tell racist jokes to describe a human being. He attended a High School that was quickly becoming more diverse, and this added tension to his worldview of race.

When he was 10, my stepfather came home complaining of a sore throat. As his fever climbed, his mother called the family doctor, who told her of this new disease plaguing young people called polio.

Polio was a life-threatening disease that could cause paralysis without constant care. As the disease progressed, my stepfather would never see the outside again for over a year as the disease ravaged his body. He would spend this time in an iron lung, a horizontal cylinder to help patients stimulate breathing to help control their respiratory muscles.

When he wasn't in the iron lung, his parents would wake him in the middle of the night to massage his joints to keep them from becoming paralyzed. My stepfather recalls these massages as grueling, painful attempts to reduce the swelling and help his strength.

In 1966, he watched parts of Omaha burn after an off-duty police officer shot a 19-year-old black male. His worldview was affirmed as the local newspaper blamed the event not on the off-duty police officer but Black people for letting their red-lined neighborhoods deteriorate.

In 1974, this man was about to meet my mother, who would remain by his side for the remainder of his life.

Before meeting him, my mother was married to my biological father, a police officer who should have faced multiple charges for abusing her and my siblings. However, his department chose to turn a blind eye both during these beatings and when they were reported.

Fearing for her and her children's lives and understanding no one was there to protect her or her children, my mother made the difficult decision to leave him.

Yet she is a survivor and flourished after divorcing my biological father, attaining her associate degree while working full-time and raising her 4 children at 28 years old. She lived until the age of 71. She was honored by the Governor at her funeral for her devotion to serving Veterans.

In 1976, my stepfather and mother were married. Two years later, my brothers, sister, and I sat on a couch as my stepfather asked if he could adopt us. We gladly accepted.

As you can tell, I may see my father differently than you after reading his story. It is not easy to accept parts of him that I often saw when we were together. Yet I also loved the man and respected the person who adopted 4 children who weren't his own.

My stepfather passed away in September 2022. After his death, I was tasked with cleaning out the house with other relatives and filtering through documents my mother and father had kept.

My mother kept everything, and I mean everything. Not only did I find my 1st-grade report cards, but I also discovered things like my siblings' adoption papers, which I had never read.

The adoption papers included several letters between my mother's and biological father's lawyers. Most of the letters were of procedures, yet one letter stood out. The last letter between the two lawyers was a petition by my biological father to grant my stepfather adoption in exchange for my mother letting him off the hook for years of missing child support.

In essence, he exploited his children as leverage to evade taking responsibility.

So far, you've read nothing that would give my stepfather any reason to justify his racism. I agree. I struggled to reconcile both parts of the man. One side of him was a loving, caring father, while one part thought it was acceptable to tell racist jokes.

How do you ultimately assess a man who adopted 4 children but grappled with his own demons like anyone else? I don't have the answer to that.

Yet, I wanted to revisit that term I introduced you to earlier and use in conflict management called *Dialectical Thinking*. It involves examining and reconciling contradictory perspectives - like your Uncle's positive personality traits and his not-so-great traits, which show up on Thanksgiving.

This is the complexity of being a human.

One of the ways to put dialectical thinking into use is by utilizing the "And Technique." It does not give someone a free pass for the negative aspects of their personality, yet it may help promote a dialogue to understanding. It may also help you release a lot of anger and frustration you feel towards that other person.

The "And Technique" basically states this: each of us is a paradox of unique characteristics. Some of these characteristics are good, and some... not so much. Using the word "and" allows us to humanize that person to create a more tolerant mindset.

This technique also allows you to de-escalate those triggers, like a MAGA hat or something else that may give you inadequate distortions of that person. When you sense that trigger, understand that you're not seeing the whole person.

For example, my "And" sentence about my stepfather is, 'My father struggled with racism, AND he was a terrific father who adopted 4 children." This technique is helpful because it allows me to think about the whole person. This doesn't absolve him of the aspects of his personality that weren't positive, but it acknowledges the credit he deserves for the things he accomplished as a human being.

Make sense?

Let's do one more. This time, we'll use that crazy Uncle who sits across from us on Thanksgiving and annoys you with his conspiracy theories.

Think about this statement about our crazy Uncle:

My Uncle and I disagree politically. I become angry when my uncle discounts my political beliefs.

AND

I appreciate that he served our country. I respect that he volunteers twice a month at the local animal shelter. I know he's been lonely since losing his wife, and is doing his best, just like me.

Remember, to see him as human, you must disconnect assigning his identity solely on his political beliefs. Our goal isn't to change his political outlook since we know that's virtually impossible. Our goal is to think about that person as a human, just like you, doing the best they can. It takes the venom out of our interactions.

So now it's your turn.

Who do you know that you disagree with politically yet still want to be part of their life? Your son or daughter? A friend? Your mother or father? Your spouse? (Yikes, that one would be especially tough).

This could even be someone you don't speak with anymore because anger got the best of you both. That's okay. We're not stuck in the past.

Complete this statement:

My (friend/spouse/son/daughter/etc.) and I disagree about

____.

AND

I appreciate this about them

____

I know they're doing the best they can, just like me.

Does that help with any internal conflicts you have with someone? I hope so.

Let me offer another experiment that may help shed some misconceptions you have about another person.

Sometimes, art can be used to help us accept differences amongst ourselves. I want to turn you on to an incredible French artist named JR, who helped me see a different view of a picture I once saw of his.

You may know JR's projects from war-torn areas around the world, the Olympics, and other projects featured in major cities like New York, Paris, Tokyo, and other locations worldwide.

One of the most profound projects JR created was simply titled, "Portrait of a Generation." This was a black and white photo of a group of children that included a young man holding a video camera resembling how someone commonly points a rifle, aimed directly at the viewer.

I'd like to get your take on this photo, so join me in this social art experiment designed to help us grapple with our own misconceptions about someone's story.

Google the picture 'JR/Portrait of a Generation' and think about what you see before you read my thoughts.

Did you do it? Great, then read on.

At first glance, it appears to be just a bunch of kids on the street having fun. But like most of his works, there was much more to the picture, which you may not understand if you simply viewed the picture without any narration. The reaction and subsequent misconception you had may have been similar to your first reaction of viewing someone with that 'Make America Great' hat or 'Black Lives Matter' shirt.

So think about your first reaction to this photo - then read the inspiration for it below.

JR took this picture in 2005 as riots broke out in the Paris suburbs. During the riots, cars were torched, buildings were set on fire, and one life was lost. Like most uprisings, embers burn hot until one event catapults it to boil over. And this is exactly what happened in France in the fall of 2005.

These riots triggered outrage after two boys, Bouna Traore, and Zyed Benna, were accidentally electrocuted in a substation while hiding from police.

The outrage and subsequent violence and destruction were not a result of this event. It stemmed from years of negative racial stereotypes and reported discrimination cases amongst France's immigrant population.

I listened to a podcast that included JR years after this picture was taken, and the podcaster had a great perspective. She asked JR if he could comment on the picture, but he hesitated to answer. JR allows us to interpret the picture through our own lens, not his.

In this famous picture, the podcaster said the message seemed to be saying, "You see us as violent street kids, but you should turn the camera and see what we see." Once I delved into the narration of the photograph, the time it was captured, and the events that shaped it, my perception of the picture shifted significantly.

And that's exactly what we don't do when we stereotype someone, whether it's a hat, shirt, or something more. We don't see the perspective of the other person.

Let's return to the earlier question: What do you think about seeing someone wearing a MAGA hat or a Black Lives Matter shirt?

I wanted to offer my own experiment to see if we were really as divided as the media portrayed us during Donald Trump's Presidency from 2016 to 2020.

Every day on Facebook I watched two close friends of political views battle it out over social media. After a while, I was fed up and ready to see if they could change their ways. I wanted to take action.

So I wondered what would happen if I brought people with different political beliefs together for a common cause? Would violence break out, or would these people work through their differences? I began the experiment just like any other social experiment, wondering how to get a group of people who don't know each other to interact with each other.

I decided I could accomplish this by starting a group on Meetup.com called "Republicans and Democrats Who Volunteer Together." I know it's not a funny or unique name like many other groups on that site, yet I wanted those who joined to clearly understand the purpose.

As I was creating the group, I wondered if anyone would be crazy enough to join.

When I hit the "Start Group" button, I worried my experiment would fail. I mean, why would complete strangers who don't know each other on different sides of the political fence want to spend a couple of hours with political rivals?

I turned on the television to catch up on some streaming and waited. After the first hour, one person joined. It was only one person - but my face lit up. Was this a mistake? Had they joined by accident?

Yet my group's numbers increased as the evening continued. I was glued to my computer, watching the numbers. There were 2 people, then 5, then 20 by the time I went to bed.

When I woke up the next day, I had 22 people in my group!

The group's political makeup includes Republicans, Democrats, Independents, those with no political beliefs, and, I'm pretty sure, a few anarchists. (It's not a requirement to state your political beliefs when joining the group - yet some self-disclose after we get to know each other.)

Our first event was at a local food bank, which was magical. There were people of different political beliefs working together to help our community.

My learning point was this: I may not have much in common politically with the guy next to me wearing the MAGA hat, yet we can both share a passion for helping our community and country.

We are not unlike other countries that have been ripped apart by political division. The truth that we share more in common with each other is affirmed by the work done by a brilliant man named Tim Phillips of the organization *"Beyond Conflict."* You may have read about Tim in my introduction. Tim has been bringing people together from conflicts in Northern Ireland to post-apartheid South

Africa and I strongly recommend reading his book to help re-establish your faith in humanity.

I hope my social experiment has motivated you to think differently about the person you see next to you. Understand that it's possible to like someone, even form a close friendship with them, even though they hold vastly different views than you do.

I teach more strategies to help us become less polarized in my class on conflict transformation. Feel free to visit our website for more information.[107]

Whew, give yourself some love after that. You can now handle the most challenging part of the conflict: managing your reactions and accepting the humanity in others.

But how do you converse with someone who is far different politically from you?

You've seen plenty of clips on YouTube that make you believe having a constructive political conversation with someone is a mythical creature, like the Chupacabra or Bigfoot. Yet, in the next chapter, we'll tear this myth to shreds and show you the almost impossible way to fail with political conversations.

Like previous chapters, they'll be in micro-lesson format for easier integration. (We Learning and Development professionals are also magical.)

---

[107] http://www.coachingforevolution.com

Chapter 10

The (Almost) Impossible Way to Fail at Political Conversations

The modern conflict strategy looks like this: avoid confrontation at all costs. If you've offended a friend, you're more likely to get a text than an invitation to a real conversation. Easier yet, they just unfriend you on Facebook as their primary strategy to let you know you've done something wrong in their eyes.

When writing this book, I had to admit something difficult: I unfollowed my father on multiple social media platforms. In my defense, my father was very political, and I don't enjoy reading hateful posts from either side of the political spectrum.

How many of you have found yourselves in similar situations with close relatives (if in a public space, be careful about randomly raising your hand unless you're that person who loves to freak out the general public). I can't help but think that this is a common occurrence.

However, it raises the question: Why do we avoid having these important conversations?

There's a valid rationale behind our hesitation to engage in these conversations: Many of us were raised in families where effective communication around challenging topics wasn't well-practiced.

Now don't be too harsh on your parents, this miscommunication cycle was probably passed down from their parents.

I probably had the same family dynamics as yours when it came to discussing sensitive subjects. For example, my father's frequent response to personal pleas like using the car was "Michael, this is not a democratic family. I'm the dictator, so no you can't use the car."

We carry this baggage of being unable to effectively discuss difficult subjects into our adult lives. How my father handled conflict was the way I handled conflict in my earlier years. To make matters worse, I used to avoid having difficult conversations in my professional and personal life, which often led to disastrous results.

Being unable to discuss difficult subjects is one of the emotional pandemics of our society. It's also one of the primary reasons you may feel our country is so polarized right now.

That's where Conflict Managers and other practitioners can assist. We're the superheroes of human conflict without the cape. (Although a cape sure would be cool to wear in my workshops.)

I'm passionate about teaching people how to resolve conflict better because I was so bad at it, and we have no chance of healing our nation unless we can learn to communicate with each other.

Hopefully, this change starts today with you.

For some people, learning how to better handle difficult conversations has life-changing benefits that can benefit their personal and business careers.

Many people lose control of their emotions and often regret what they say not because they're bad people but because they simply haven't learned strategies for handling difficult conversations. Think about how you feel after a bad argument. Once you learn how to gain control in conflict, you gain that power back.

Second, these conflict management tips aren't just isolated for political conversations. They can be used to improve interpersonal conflicts in relationships, with roommates, and even with your dog (if your dog argues with you).

Following my conflict transformation workshops, I've had many people express gratitude for providing them with a framework for engaging in more constructive conversations. They applied this framework to re-establish contact with someone they hadn't spoken to in several years and initiate a dialogue with them. Sometimes the sheer relief on their faces is priceless.

The first tip on your road to strengthening these conversations comes to you from Kwame Christian from the American Negotiation Institute. Kwame partnered with the United Nations, where his team teaches Nigerian youths how to use negotiation and conflict transformation to change their communities.[108]

Raise your hand if arguing was your family's way of handling conflict. (Again, if you're having coffee in a public place, feel free to just raise your eyebrows instead of your hand so people don't think you're strange).

Kwame's first tip is learning the difference between arguing and conflict resolution: *Conflict resolution is not about winning.*

You may have learned in your family dynamic that disagreeing was about doing what it took to make sure you were heard, so you shouted louder and louder until you felt the other person heard you.

---

[108] Erica Thompson, "Negotiation Expert Kwame Christian Is on a Mission to Change the World," The Columbus Dispatch, April 4, 2022, https://www.dispatch.com/story/business/2022/01/20/american-negotiation-institute-founder-kwame-christian-mission/8749470002/.

If you were loud enough or lucky enough to get the last word, you may have thought you won.

Winning though came at a cost. At times, winning meant you said hurtful things to punish the other person for not listening to you. Hurting someone else emotionally is not winning.

Additionally, what does compliance look like from the other person even if you feel you won by using these tactics? It's human nature to want to get back at the other person if you feel you've lost an argument. So, the unwritten treaty you've agreed to with that other person is not an effective agreement.

So, the first tip is we need to learn that conflict is not about "winning."

So, how do we get past this?

The next tip in any conflict transformation is so powerful that it deserves its own book. We discussed the concept previously when you were learning about dialectical thinking.

Tip #2 comes directly from the talented author and storyteller Brene Brown in her conversation rules: "In order to empathize with someone's experience, you must believe them as they see it, and not how you imagine their experience to be."

If the other person disagrees with you they may actually believe what they're telling you is correct. Transformation has little chance of occurring unless you accept that fact.

So the next time someone disagrees with you, take 3 seconds to lower your energy level. Look into their eyes, listen to their point of view, and possibly even feel their pain or anger. Accepting them as imperfect may allow you to see them, perhaps for the first time, as humans. You begin to accept them for the fact that they really do believe what they're thinking.

And thank them for their answer.

The easiest way for another person to see the good in you is to see the good in them. If they see the good in you, that you're sincerely trying to connect and get past the hurt, they'll want you to see the good in them.

Don't push them away with your hate. Pull them in with your peace.

Sitting people down at a table across from each other and utilizing this type of strategy is exactly why mediators like Tim Phillips have been able to help people from places like South Africa, Northern Ireland, and other war-ravaged countries.

The next benefit of learning better conflict management skills is gaining power over conflict instead of allowing conflict to have control over you.

You may have learned valuable skills that took time to grow. For example, you may be a coding guru. You may have learned how to be a great parent, smart financially, or someone who creates funny social media posts. You worked on that skill because it was important to you.

Improving conflict transformation grows when you practice. It's OK if you're not great when you start, I promise you'll get better with more experience. Think about the tremendous benefactors you'll gain: better relationships, more work opportunities, and self-confidence.

Not sure where to start? We have you covered.

Start small with some simple "I" statements (it's the opposite of its evil twin - the "you" statement which sometimes gets a phone thrown at you). "I" statements facilitate effective communication by making others more receptive to your perspective.

The technique looks like this:

"I feel (place emotion here) when (explanation)." What I would appreciate is (explain) to help me feel less (emotion)".

Let's say you're increasingly annoyed by your friend's cell phone usage when you're trying to discuss something important with them.

Your conversation might sound like this:

"I feel annoyed when I'm trying to communicate with you and you're on the phone. What I would appreciate is if you put your phone down when I communicate so I feel less annoyed."

Pro Tip: Watch your energy level before making your "I" statement - calm down before having this conversation, even if you need a minute to do this, or this may also get the phone thrown at you.

How would you use the "I" statement to tell someone you don't appreciate their negative political statements?

We wrote earlier how conflict management is just like any other skill - it's a contact sport, and you'll get better with practice. You get good at it through exposure therapy.

Think about it: We're willing to invest $15 a month in a Netflix subscription but are unwilling to invest time in learning how to become better at resolving conflicts. So, right now, while you're thinking about it, capture this winning "I" formula above on your phone, tablet, or paper so you can access it when needed.

But what about deeper conversations? Like the conversation you'd like to have with someone you've broken off a personal relationship with because you both became heated about a political view or some other issue?

We use a 4-Part Success Formula which targets the emotional baggage and seeks to replace it with a new shared reality between both parties.

There are 4 parts to the Conflict Transformation Success Formula:

1. Preparation
2. Opening
3. Discussion
4. and Follow-Up.

While most of my clients focus on the discussion step, they often underestimate the other stages of the conflict transformation success formula. They can't understand why the other person doesn't "get it" that they are trying to help.

We'll show you how to approach all four areas. By the way, this conversation model can be used for most conflicts, not just political disagreements.

The four parts of the conversation are all independent variables, yet success depends on using all the steps.

Let's learn about Step One:

Step 1:

Preparation for the Conversation by Establishing Conversation Rules and an Irresistible Invitation to Talk

How many of you had the best intentions of resolving a conflict with someone only to have it go sideways? The answer to this question is everyone. Even your best intentions for a positive conversation can quickly go wrong if you start the conversation without recognizing the other person may go on the attack and you're not sure how to emotionally defend yourself.

Think about why we teach children the importance of looking for cars when they cross a street - we want to provide a framework so they can understand what's expected of them. Most importantly we want to keep them safe.

So prior to the conversation, create a simple list of conversation rules. These rules benefit both people by creating a safe space. The boundaries should be clear and can be individualized for each person. For example, you may need more personal space than the other person, or they may not be fond of talking in coffee shops. Get those details out of the way first.

Common Conversation Agreements Include:

- Agree that both people are doing the best they can
- Agree that the conversation is about moving forward - not reliving prior problems
- Wait for the other person to finish talking before starting
- No yelling or verbal abuse
- Use "I" statements instead of "you" statements (you'll read about this technique later)
- It's okay to disagree, it's not ok to make the other person feel guilty for disagreeing
- It's okay at any time to take a break if needed

I recall a conversation I had with a former supervisor following my unsuccessful application for a promotion. During that conversation, I realized how these agreements could have been quite beneficial. The supervisor had genuine intentions to discuss my disappointment, yet it went quickly sideways as I had suspicions about how she was promoted within the company.

At the beginning of the meeting, she raised excellent ideas on how I could improve myself for the next opportunity. However, my mindset entering the meeting wasn't focused on making progress; instead, it was centered around finding ways to express my frustration. I had already broken the first two points of the conversation agreements listed above by not giving my supervisor the benefit of the doubt by asking about my response to the promotion I didn't receive.

One of my remarks got personal during the conversation - I knew my supervisor had been quickly promoted prior to my employment there. She also had a sister in upper management. During the conversation, I offered input that was unwelcome.

"It seems like anyone with relatives in upper management gets promoted with no questions asked," I said defensively.

Ouch.

In your career, there are CLM's (Career Limiting Moves) and CEM's (Career Ending Moves) that you create for yourself. Both limiting moves are self-induced. Guess which one that comment led to?

It just goes to show that many who enter a field do so for self-improvement - and learning how to better understand and improve my reactions was one of the primary reasons I entered the field of conflict management.

So what happens when you approach a conversation aimed at resolving differences with good intentions, but the other person appears determined to demonstrate your perceived wrongness?

Many times this results in a wider rift between the two people. Some just give up speaking with the other person, at times for years.

Let's analyze what may have happened and learn how to approach it more effectively.

You were ready and willing to have the conversation to mend fences with the other person, but you probably didn't realize how important setting the stage was to a good outcome. Remember what we said earlier. Just because you are ready to move forward doesn't mean the other person is. Everyone needs to feel they have a safe landing zone before they even think about having a difficult conversation.

Here's one of the best conflict management hacks I've learned to prepare for a conversation. It's from the person I mentioned earlier, United Nations negotiator Kwame Christian, author of the book, "Finding Confidence in Conflict." The secret is to make the invitation so exceedingly positive that there's no way that person can refuse your invitation. The hack's scientific potency lies in its ability to create a safe haven within the other person's neocortex, enabling them to lower their defenses and engage in a productive conversation.

The conversation might look like this:

"Emma, I want to thank you for being a friend of mine in good times, as well as times I really needed someone by my side. I haven't always been able to count on someone being there, but you never wavered, and I wanted to tell you how much I appreciate that." (*Make sure you wait for a response*).

Ok, so far so good, right?

Next comes the invitation. Be specific about wanting to bridge the divide and offer a specific time to meet. Asking for a specific time is important so "life" doesn't get in the way and delay the heart-to-heart.

Here's how the next part might sound:

"I know we've become distant in the last couple of years, and I sincerely want us to get back on track of being good friends. Which way you lean politically doesn't matter to me. What does matter is our friendship. I know I've caught you off guard, and I'd like us to be in a better place in the future. Let's work on this together. How does meeting this Thursday at 3 at (insert favorite location here) sound to get us back on track?"

Who couldn't resist saying yes to this invite?

Did you catch the other powerful NLP wording we used? The invite leverages the power of the future, which forces them to look ahead instead of backward.

By the way, I want to add something to this invite in case it applies to you. Sometimes participants approached me after a class and said they were to blame for the relationship becoming toxic. They didn't handle an argument well or know how to bridge the gap. So they employed the "hope strategy" of not doing anything and 'hoping' that time just solved the issue. It usually didn't.

If this applies to you, including an apology is an absolutely critical element needed in the invitation. Many people forgive in stages, and apologizing is an essential first step, so include it as part of your invite.

If you've had volatile or hostile conversations in the past, include your suggested Conversation Agreements you learned about earlier here. Never point the finger when suggesting these agreements, instead, allow them to suggest what agreements are important to them.

For example, "I really want us to move forward, so what conversation agreements would make this easier for you?" Thank them for any conversation agreements they offer, it now makes it easier to respond with your conversation agreements important to you.

Okay, so you've contacted your friend, and they've agreed to your request– great!

Some backsliding may appear from your friend here. Your friend may text and say they're anxious and unsure if this is the best move for them. That's okay. Hesitation is perfectly natural. Even though you've mentally moved forward, remember that they are just now uncovering a wound and are uncertain if they want to rip off the emotional Band-Aid.

Try to put yourself in the other person's shoes by recalling your own friendship difficulties. Have you ever felt unsure if you should accept your friend's request to hash out your differences? What do you do when you see their name pop up on your phone? Reassure them that you are committed to having a polite conversation and remind them how important they are to you.

Let's head to Step 2 if they're ready to move on.

Step 2:
Opening

Make sure you approach the conversation in a distraction-free setting. Put your phone away and find a place to talk semi-privately. Your friend should be your sole focus.

You might assume that starting a conversation is the simplest part, but it can quickly take a wrong turn because strong emotions haven't been addressed yet. Here are some best practices for get started, which I call the 'Compliment Sandwich' (credit given to Ted Lasso):

Thank the person again for meeting you. If you owe them an apology, reiterate that as well. This simple reassurance and apology lowers their 'fight or flight' trigger, which you learned about in the previous chapter.

Step 3:
Discussion

You're now ready to move on to the heart of the matter. There will be many feelings that bubble to the surface, including some areas you're sensitive about. Keep in mind that once you've discussed these matters, you'll be ready to progress, so consider how much you genuinely want to move forward and strive to ensure that the conversation aims to repair relationships rather than "win" an argument. Using the Conversation Path below can help you stay on track:

The Conversation Path:
Ask – Listen and Reflect – Agree and Move Forward.

This path was created by one of my favorite resources for conflict management titled 'Difficult Conversations," a book by Bruce Patton and Sheila Heen of the Harvard Negotiation Project.

Ask

Asking questions will help them feel heard and lower their defenses. The purpose of these questions is to help both of you work through the emotional component and the problem. Many times, the emotional component and the problem are not related to each other. In fact, sometimes, my clients have even forgotten about why they were upset in the first place. They've created a false narrative about what they believe the other person did. In time, that small dilemma becomes gigantic in their mind.

Here are some great probing questions to help you discuss the issue(s):

> "You're important to me. What can I do differently the next time to make you feel better and meet your needs?"

> "Tell me about what you're feeling now."
>
> "You're important to me. Tell me what I can do in the future to handle this better."

Listen and Reflect

Use non-verbal and verbal queues to let them know you're engaged and interested in their words. If you've ever been to a counselor with another person, you'll probably remember that one of the primary benefits of having them present is to make sure people get heard.

Do not interject. This is not the time to prove you were right (even if you believe you were).

Here are some things to help them understand that you're listening:

> "So, I heard you say…"
>
> "I understand. Thank you for sharing."

Whew! You've made it this far. Let's take it home now.

Here are some ways to know that your friend is ready to move forward:

- Nonverbal signals like smiling and uncrossed arms.
- Statements like "I'm so glad we're talking again."

Share Your Story

This is now the time to share your story to ensure your voice is heard. Tell them how you felt without accusations.

"Thank you for sharing your story. I appreciate your input. Can I offer some ways it personally affected me as well?"

"When we drifted apart, it hurt that we couldn't talk."

"I was upset at the way it ended."

Some participants in my workshops ask why they wait so long to address their needs. In my workshops, we learn about the law of reciprocity. (It's actually used in sales conversations all the time - you may not have been aware of it.)

The Law of Reciprocity says that if you provide something of value, you have unconsciously or consciously established the right to request something from the other person. (Recall when you buy a new car that they usually ask for a review after they've handed you the keys.)

It's perfectly okay to address your needs earlier if you feel it's the right time, yet remembering this law usually makes them more open to listening to your needs. Remember, they may have never learned how to properly resolve personal conflicts in their family, and they carry that baggage into their adult lives, just like any baggage you're carrying.

You've reached the final part of the conversation.

Agree and Move Forward

Here are some statements that help migrate you and your friend to the final part of the conversation.

> "I'm so glad we're having this talk. I feel
>
> ____."
>
> "How do you feel?"

> "Tell me what we could do together to help move us forward?"

Okay, you've finished the conversation. You sense you and your friend are on a better path toward positive communication. You're ready to move forward. Now what's next?

Step 4:
Follow-up and Plan for Potholes

How many of you believe that the problem you discussed has been completely resolved? I know I wish I had better news, but you've already guessed what comes next. Anyone living in cold, snowy locations that have equally uncomfortable hot summers understands that potholes appeal every year. These dreaded concrete craters have the ability to throw both your car and your day off course. The same goes for your tenuous reconciliation.

I call this post-conversation phenomenon that sometimes occurs "The Pothole Effect" when problems resurface. Yet, keep in mind these are only bumps in the road - know they are a natural part of the healing process.

Consider these items to minimize the pothole effect for your follow-up plan. Please adjust the wording for your situation:

- Communicate what you agreed on with a quick text or phone call. "Thank you so much for yesterday! I want to make sure I fully understand your needs. We discussed_______________ and ___________________. What else did you want to make sure I understood? (After they respond) Great, thank you. I also wanted to re-communicate my needs were ____________ and ___________.

- Follow through on any action items.
- Check-in as needed.

Your journey to patch things up with a friend who you've become distanced from or had a long-standing disagreement with may be different. If this person is important to you, try this conflict management strategy we've discussed. You may be surprised at how much better you feel, and I promise it could lead to small steps that could transform your relationship.

I'm going to leverage my nerdy learning tools now.

How would you like to self-practice having a difficult conversation before actually going live?

We've included a link to the "Angry Uncle" chatbot on our website, created by Karin Tamerius, which simulates some of the material we've covered. You get to choose whether the Uncle is left-leaning or right-leaning. If you're an Independent, Anarchist, or just want to have more civil conversations, try both sides of the conversation!

Don't forget about the worksheet we've included on our website to help guide you through these conversations.[109]

By the way, I want to applaud you if this has inspired you to engage in a challenging conversation that you've been avoiding. Improving relationships is good for your mental health. It also serves the dual purpose of improving our democracy.

Try some of these conversation tools (or at least visit our Angry Uncle bot, which is pretty cool) before heading onto the final chapter.

---

[109] Go to www.coachingforevolution.com for more guidance and resources.

Chapter 11

Thinking Old Democracy and Re-Thinking New Democracy – A New Hope

In the spring of 2023, I took a short vacation to Monument Valley, a red-sand desert on the Arizona-Utah border. The valley is a sacred place to the Navajo Nation, and it's easy to see why. My wife and I watched as the sun dipped over the horizon, bathing the desert in crimson and gold.

This trip had been on my bucket list for years, but I could've never imagined how the experience would affect me.

The highlight of the vacation was a spiritual tour through this revered land led by a young Navajo guide.

During the tour, our guide took us to some of the most sacred places his community cherished. The areas were well-preserved and contained petroglyphs that told stories passed down through the generations. Even though many of his relatives had passed, their messages to our guide lived on in these special mountains.

He took us to Big Hogan Arch, a cave with a natural arch eroded in the sandstone. The bluff is angled inward, allowing you to lean back while standing up so you can gaze at the top of it.

While peering up, the colors of this arch magically formed the perfect shape of an eagle's head, while the hole in the arch formed the shape of the eagle's eye.

Our guide spoke of his community's belief in shared respect and reverence for one another.

At this bluff, he asked that we power off our cell phones and contemplate the positive experiences that goodness could generate for us and others in our lives. During this reflective time, I recalled the wise words he mentioned earlier on our tour, "When we talk about moving forward, it really means we're going back to our roots."

Our guide was incredibly proud of his ancestors, and it made me wonder what our generation's ancestors would say to us if they could speak to us now.

If they could speak to us now, I believe most of our ancestors would offer a message of hope. Like us, they lived in challenging times. Many of our ancestors fought wars, tolled long hours in horrible working conditions, and protested for equality so that we could enjoy a better life than they did.

Like the Navajo, I believe the messages our ancestors are trying to communicate to us are all around - we just have to be open to receiving them.

The shepherd's heart and the proud warrior spirit of Navajo Chief Manuelito are channeled in the Navajo guide who treated me to a tour of his sacred lands.

I see the continued fire for equal rights and justice in speeches by Yolanda Renee King, granddaughter of Martin Luther King and Coretta Scott King.

I recognize the sense of duty to better the world in my grandfather, Henry Lee, who risked his life fighting against human atrocities in World War II, and in my mother, who was an early advocate for women's rights. This sense of purpose also resonates in me.

I hope you can recognize the calling you may now be having to help improve our country and world for future generations.

Our political ancestors never envisioned a democracy that didn't change with the times; they were clear that future generations get to decide what our country's democracy looks like. I believe they're channeling that message to us now.

I hope you saw some of the roads that can get us there in my book, from better representation in our political elections to eliminating corporate influence on our politicians. They will represent monumental evolution in our democracy so future generations can finally say the power of the United States is within "all of us," not "some of us."

Additionally, I hope you recognize that our biggest evolution in the country won't take place in Washington, but perhaps within yourself first, learning to accept others.

It's time to look in the eyes of the person with a different worldview from you and see the whole person, not just the views you disagree with. They are people who experience both triumphs and challenges in their human journey, much like yourself.

We have invested too much in the forces that divide our nation – and our youngest generations are paying too great a cost for our division.

Our pride, regardless of which political party you lean towards, shouldn't have to be our children's burden.

Dan Millman wrote, "The secret to change is to focus all of your energy, not in fighting the old, but on building the new". That 'new' democracy our youngest generations envision only exists if we have the courage to work together.

Lend your voice and join a dedicated community driven to help peacefully build this new democracy and move it forward.

Until we meet again, my friends, I wish you good health, peace, much love, and hope.

Welcome to the Evolution.

Acknowledgments

I have giants of "Revolution Science" whom I need to thank for guiding me in this book. One of these experts is a rock star in this field...Barbara F. Walter, who has written for the Washington Post, and Wall Street. Journal. She ventured into troubled areas to document the source of many of her findings.

I also have to thank the late Ted Gurr, Jack A. Goldstone, and Erica Chenoweth for their incredible contributions as pioneers in revolution science. By studying the past they have revealed future possible roadmaps of hope for our country. Without such bravery and science, we would be further off knowing what elements cause disruptions in the world.

I want to give thanks and credit to authors Eric Liu and Jamie Margolin who inspired me to create this checklist. I appreciate you and thank you for your guidance.

I want to thank my wife who undoubtedly is the best human I've ever known. I thank you for your support and am honored and grateful to be your husband. I wake and smile each morning knowing you are my partner in life Blue Eyes 1.

Finally, I want to thank some of our wisest citizens, our newest voting generation, for your insight and contribution to this book. Many of us walk alongside you and are fighting the good fight with you. We resist because you exist.

Note: My linktree site: https://linktr.ee/evolutionrevolutionnow, summarizes each chapter of this book. You'll also find references to helpful resources, including self-exercises and more. I would also encourage you to subscribe to one of my favorite podcasts, "How to Citizen." In this podcast, Baratunde Thurston offers unique insights on how to be better citizens and hope for future generations.

Bibliography

1. Frank, Jerome D. Sanity and survival in the Nuclear Age: Psychological Aspects of war and peace. Random House, 1987.

2. As of this publication, Twitter is now known as "X." For continuity, we will call it Twitter throughout.

3. Lima, Cristiano. "Analysis | Jan. 6 Panel Spotlights Twitter's Role in Insurrection." The Washington Post, July 13, 2022. https://www.washingtonpost.com/politics/2022/07/13/jan-6-panel-spotlights-twitter-role-insurrection/.

4. "Political Instability Task Force." Wikipedia, August 19, 2022. https://en.wikipedia.org/wiki/Political_Instability_Task_Force#:~:text=The%20PITF%20first%20identified%20over,changes%2C%20and%20genocides%20and%20politicides.

5. Allen, Mike. "Record Number of Americans Say They're Politically Independent - Axios." Axios. Accessed August 23, 2023. https://www.axios.com/2023/04/17/poll-americans-independent-republican-democrat.

6. Allen, 2023

7. Kochhar, Rakesh, and Stella Sechopoulos. "How the American Middle Class Has Changed in the Past Five Decades." Pew Research Center, April 21, 2022. https://www.pewresearch.

org/short-reads/2022/04/20/how-the-american-middle-class-has-changed-in-the-past-five-decades/.

8. Dickler, Jessica. "Amid Inflation, More Middle-Class Americans Struggle to Make Ends Meet." CNBC, January 18, 2023. https://www.cnbc.com/2023/01/18/amid-inflation-more-middle-class-americans-struggle-to-make-ends meet.html#:~:text=The%20middle%20class%20is%20shrinking&text=As%20is%20often%20cited%2C%20the,years%20earlier%2C%20according%20to%20Pew.

9. "Young People's Ambivalent Relationship with Political Parties." Circle at Tufts, October 24, 2018. https://circle.tufts.edu/latest-research/young-peoples-ambivalent-relationship-political-parties.

10. J. E. SPENCE, Book Reviews, Community Development Journal, Volume 7, Issue 3, October 1972, Pages 199–200, https://doi.org/10.1093/cdj/7.3.199

11. Walter, Barbara F. How Civil Wars Start: And How To Stop Them. London, UK: Penguin Books, 2023. Journalism Project, June 7, 2023.

12. Clevenger, Andrew. "DC Guard Chief Details Pentagon Delays during Jan. 6 Riot at Capitol." Roll Call, March 3, 2021. https://rollcall.com/2021/03/03/d-c-guard-chief-details-pentagon-delays-during-jan-6-riot-at-capitol/.

13. Cole, Brendan. "Mike Pence Hid in 'Loading Dock' in Parking Garage during January 6 Riot." Newsweek, November 9, 2021. https://www.newsweek.com/mike-pence-january-6-riot-loading-dock-underground-parking-garage-1647353.

14. Nietzel, Michael T. 2023. "A New Seton Hall University Report Profiles the People Prosecuted for January 6

Insurrection." Forbes. Forbes Magazine. July 31, 2023. https://www.forbes.com/sites/michaeltnietzel/2023/07/28/a-new-seton-hall-university-report-profiles-the-people-prosecuted-for-january-6-insurrection/?sh=28bfb900722b.

15. Phillips, Timothy, Mary Albon, Ina Breuer, David Taffel, Václav Havel, David Ervine, and Leonel Gómez. Beyond Conflict: The Project On Justice In Times of Transition: 20 Years Of Putting Experience To Work For Peace. Cambridge, MA: Project on Justice in Times of Transition, 2013.

16. "Ignaz Semmelweis," Wikipedia, August 21, 2023, https://en.wikipedia.org/wiki/Ignaz_Semmelweis#Breakdown_and_death.

17. Wash Your Hands! Survey- https://www.surveymonkey.com/r/8ZQHDYZ

18. "American Revolution Facts." American Battlefield Trust, August 24, 2021. http://battlefields.org/learn/articles/american-revolution-faqs#:~:text=Throughout%20the%20course%20of%20the%20war%2C%20an%20estimated%206%2C800%20Americans,died%20while%20prisoners%20of%20war).

19. Robson, David. "The '3.5% Rule': How a Small Minority Can Change the World." BBC Future, March 3, 2023. https://www.bbc.com/future/article/20190513-it-only-takes-35-of-people-to-change-the-world.

20. Middleton, Jess. "The Trendline - Global Political Risk at Highest Level in Five Years." Verisk Maplecroft, February 2, 2023. https://www.maplecroft.com/insights/analysis/risk-signals-global-political-risk-at-highest-level-in-five-years/.

21. "Assistance Association for Political Prisoners." Assistance Association for Political Prisoners. Accessed August 23, 2023. https://aappb.org/.

22. Green, Lindsay. "'Our Health Workers Are Working in Fear': After Myanmar's Military Coup, One Year of Targeted Violence against Health Care." PHR, January 28, 2022. https://phr.org/our-work/resources/one-year-anniversary-of-the-myanmar-coup-detat/.

23. Gurr, Ted Robert. Essay. In Why Men Rebel, 24-25. London: Routledge, Taylor & Francis Group, 2016.

24. Carothers, Thomas. 2023. "Is the Global Tide Turning in Favor of Democracy?" Carnegie Endowment for International Peace. May 30, 2023. https://carnegieendowment.org/2023/05/30/is-global-tide-turning-in-favor-of-democracy-pub-89838.

25. Walter, 24.

26. Gurr, 24-25.

27. "From Democracy to Dictatorship." RDI, August 21, 2023. https://rdi.org/articles/from-democracy-to-dictatorship/.

28. Chamorro-Premuzic, Tomas. "Why Do so Many Incompetent Men Become Leaders?" Harvard Business Review, February 27, 2023. https://hbr.org/2013/08/why-do-so-many-incompetent-men.

29. Judah, Ben. "How Putin Plunged Russia toward Totalitarianism." Slate Magazine, March 10, 2022. https://slate.com/news-and-politics/2022/03/putin-russia-totalitarianism-soviet-style-oppression.html.

30. "Ukraine War: US Estimates 200,000 Military Casualties on All Sides." BBC News, November 10, 2022. https://www.bbc.com/news/world-europe-63580372.

31. "Ukraine: Civilian Casualty Update 31 July 2023." OHCHR, July 31, 2023. https://www.ohchr.org/en/news/2023/07/ukraine-civilian-casualty-update-31-july-2023#:~:text=Total%20civilian%20casualties,9%2C369%20killed%20and%2016%2C646%20injured.

32. "The Putin Critics Who Have Been Assassinated." Sky News. Accessed August 23, 2023. https://news.sky.com/story/the-putin-critics-who-have-been-assassinated-10369350.

33. TYSHCHENKO, KATERYNA. "Wagner Group Now Just 400 Km Away from Moscow." Ukrainska Pravda, June 24, 2023. https://www.pravda.com.ua/eng/news/2023/06/24/7408365/.

34. Kedia, Gayannée, Thomas Mussweiler, and David E J Linden. "Brain Mechanisms of Social Comparison and Their Influence on the Reward System." Neuroreport, November 12, 2014. https://www.ncbi.nlm.nih.gov/pmc/articles/PMC4222713/.

35. "Ukraine War: US Estimates 200,000 Military Casualties on All Sides." BBC News, November 10, 2022. https://www.bbc.com/news/world-europe-63580372.

36. "Ted Robert Gurr." AAPSS, May 4, 2023. https://www.aapss.org/fellow/ted-robert-gurr/.

37. Gurr, 24-25.

38. OECD (2019), Under Pressure: The Squeezed Middle Class, OECD Publishing, Paris https://doi.org/10.1787/689afed1-en

39. Alcantara, Chris Alcantara, Abha Bhattarai, and Andrew Van Dam. "Rents Are Rising Everywhere. See How Much Prices Are up in Your Area." The Washington Post, April 21, 2022. https://www.washingtonpost.com/business/interactive/2022/rising-rent-prices/.

40. "History of 1918 Flu Pandemic." Centers for Disease Control and Prevention, March 21, 2018. https://www.cdc.gov/flu/pandemic-resources/1918-commemoration/1918-pandemic-history.htm.

41. Zarevich, E.R. "How the Black Death Led to the Peasants' Revolt." explorethearchive.com, July 1, 2021. https://explorethearchive.com/peasants-revolt.

42. Courie, Leonard W. The Black Death and Peasant's Revolt. New York: Wayland Publishers, 1972; Strayer, Joseph R., ed. Dictionary of the Middle Ages. New York: Charles Scribner's Sons. Vol. 2. pp. 257-267.

43. Ferguson, Stephanie. "Understanding America's Labor Shortage: The Most Impacted Industries." U.S. Chamber of Commerce, August 10, 2023. https://www.uschamber.com/workforce/understanding-americas-labor-shortage-the-most-impacted-industries.

44. "Union Members Summary." US Department of Labor, January 19, 2023. Bureau of Labor and Statistics. https://www.bls.gov/news.release/union2.nr0.htm.

45. Garver, Rob. "Major Strikes Loom in US Labor Market." VOA, July 20, 2023. https://www.voanews.com/a/major-strikes-loom-in-us-labor-market-/7189659.html.

46. Robson, David. "The '3.5% Rule': How a Small Minority Can Change the World." BBC Future, March 3, 2023. https://

www.bbc.com/future/article/20190513-it-only-takes-35-of-people-to-change-the-world.

47. Panetta, Grace. "How a Rogue Governor Could Steal the Next Presidential Election for Trump." Business Insider, January 31, 2022. https://www.businessinsider.com/how-a-rogue-governor-could-steal-the-next-presidential-election-for-trump-2022-1?fbclid=IwAR3CCmIV2D0B-FRgqxb5dYPJAItUGZBGeZsKYy6U3gK9fDOUZJdiwSYxLVM.

48. Elaine Cromie. "Republicans in Michigan Have Replaced Election Officials Who Certified Biden's Win," NPR, May 4, 2022, https://www.npr.org/2022/05/04/1096641003/republicans-in-michigan-have-replaced-election-officials-who-certified-bidens-wi?fbclid=IwAR0SAGoacy4F1NCYrm2GVwNVmTZkI4edMCGNxnIg1NfwPX2gT0xyp6fY0lU.

49. Gardner, Amy, and Isaac Arnsdorf. "More than 100 GOP Primary Winners Back Trump's False Fraud Claims." The Washington Post, June 16, 2022. https://www.washingtonpost.com/politics/2022/06/14/more-than-100-gop-primary-winners-back-trumps-false-fraud-claims/.

50. "North Carolina's Gerrymandered Districts Set Stage for 2024 Republican Wins." The Guardian, May 31, 2023. https://www.theguardian.com/us-news/2023/may/31/north-carolina-gerrymander-republicans-2024-us-elections.

51. State of Arizona. House Bill 2596, page 35, lines 10-17 https://www.azleg.gov/legtext/55leg/2R/bills/HB2596P.pdf

52. Learn more about ranked-choice voting here: https://www.fairvote.org/rcv#where_is_ranked_choice_voting_used

53. Sign the petition here: https://www.nationalpopularvote.com/

54. Friedman, Lisa, and Alyssa Lukpat. "Vanessa Nakate, Speaking for a Leery Youth Movement, Offers a Challenge: 'Prove US Wrong.'" The New York Times, November 11, 2021. https://www.nytimes.com/2021/11/11/climate/vanessa-nakate-speaking-for-a-leery-youth-movement-offers-a-challenge-prove-us-wrong.html?fbclid=IwAR16YETzIkO8O-qGiWYrlMZgOYAedUyao9Z5MdLehCsDQ5_W0K7MsHeULcA.

55. Project, The Media Insight. "The News Consumption Habits of 16- to 40-Year-Olds." American Press Institute, August 31, 2022. https://www.americanpressinstitute.org/publications/reports/survey-research/the-news-consumption-habits-of-16-to-40-year-olds/.

56. Collins, Dave. "Alex Jones Ordered to Pay $473m More to Sandy Hook Families." AP News, November 10, 2022. https://apnews.com/article/entertainment-shootings-business-connecticut-alex-jones-c6d0563dc17e7bfa83a881b44e7b9eec.

57. Taylor, Kate."America's Teenagers Skew a Lot More Conservative than Most People Realize, and They Get Most of Their News from Instagram." Business Insider. Accessed August 25, 2023. https://www.businessinsider.com/gen-z-changes-political-divides-2019-7.

58. Nadeem, Reem. "Amid a Series of Mass Shootings in the U.S., Gun Policy Remains Deeply Divisive." Pew Research Center - U.S. Politics & Policy, April 28, 2022. https://www.pewresearch.org/politics/2021/04/20/amid-a-series-of-mass-shootings-in-the-u-s-gun-policy-remains-deeply-divisive/.

59. Kurtzleben, Danielle. "Why Are U.S. Elections So Much Longer than Other Countries'?" NPR, October 21, 2015. https://www.npr.org/sections/itsallpolitics/2015/10/21/450238156/canadas-11-week-campaign-reminds-us-that-american-elections-are-much-longer.

60. Montanaro, Domenico. "Super Tuesday Was Created to Nominate Someone Moderate. It Backfired." NPR, March 1, 2020. https://www.npr.org/2016/02/29/468253626/a-history-of-super-tuesday.

61. Learn more about this legalized corruption and how to fight it in this quick video: https://www.youtube.com/watch?v=5tu32CCA_Ig&t=6s

62. Bell, Peter. "Public Trust in Government: 1958-2022." Pew Research Center - U.S. Politics & Policy, August 22, 2023. https://www.pewresearch.org/politics/2022/06/06/public-trust-in-government-1958-2022/.

63. Allen, Danielle. "Opinion | The House Was Supposed to Grow with Population. It Didn't. Let's Fix That." The Washington Post, August 23, 2023. https://www.washingtonpost.com/opinions/2023/02/28/danielle-allen-democracy-reform-congress-house-expansion/.

64. "Learn How We Can Replace Career Politicians with Citizen Legislators by Enlarging the U.S. House of Representatives.," Thirty-Thousand, August 12, 2022, https://thirty-thousand.org/overview/.

65. Find out how to contact your state senator at these websites: https://thirty-thousand.org/overview/ and https://www.congress.gov/bill/118th-congress/house-bill/643?q=%7B%22search%22%3A%5B%22casten%22%5D%7D&s=2&r=24

66. Youtube video: https://youtu.be/UTP4uvIFu5c

67. "AARP Poll Finds 96 Percent Support Social Security ." AARP, August 24, 2022. https://www.aarp.org/retirement/social-security/info-2020/aarp-poll-finds-near-universal-support.html.

68. Veghte, Benjamin. "Social Security's Past, Present and Future." National Academy of Social Insurance – Advancing Solutions for Social Security, Medicare, and Medicaid, November 30, 2020. https://www.nasi.org/discussion/social-securitys-past-present-and-future/.

69. http://www.coachingforevolution.com

70. Daniel J. Levitin. Extracted from The Organized Mind: Thinking Straight in the Age of Information Overload, published by Viking. It was republished in The Guardian, January 18, 2015, https://www.theguardian.com/science/2015/jan/18/modern-world-bad-for-brain-daniel-j-levitin-organized-mind-information-overload. It was republished in The Guardian, January 18, 2015, https://www.theguardian.com/science/2015/jan/18/modern-world-bad-for-brain-daniel-j-levitin-organized-mind-information-overload.

71. Levitin, 2015.

72. Timberg, Craig, Elizabeth Dwoskin, and Reed Albergotti. "Inside Facebook, Jan. 6 Violence Fueled Anger, Regret over Missed Warning Signs." The Washington Post, October 29, 2021. https://www.washingtonpost.com/technology/2021/10/22/jan-6-capitol-riot-facebook/.

73. Timberg, 2021.

74. Bunzeck, Nico, and Emrah Düzel. "Absolute Coding of Stimulus Novelty in the Human Substantia Nigra/VTA." Neuron, August 2, 2006. https://www.sciencedirect.com/science/article/pii/S0896627306004752.

75. Eyre, Harris, Ian MacRae, and Sandi Chapman. "Social Media Is Changing Our Brains." Center for BrainHealth® The University of Texas at Dallas, December

5, 2021. https://centerforbrainhealth.org/article/social-media-is-changing-our-brains.

76. Merrill, Jeremy B., and Will Oremus. "Five Points for Anger, One for a 'Like': How Facebook's Formula Fostered Rage and Misinformation." The Washington Post, October 26, 2021. https://www.washingtonpost.com/technology/2021/10/26/facebook-angry-emoji-algorithm/.

77. Mason, Melanie. "The Mean Tweets Are Coming from inside the House. Study of Politicians' Twitter Looks at 'Civility.'" Los Angeles Times, April 28, 2022. https://www.latimes.com/politics/story/2022-04-28/twitter-incivility-up-among-members-of-congress-study-finds.

78. Gross, Justin H., and Kaylee T. Johnson. "Twitter Taunts and Tirades: Negative Campaigning in the Age of Trump: PS: Political Science & Politics." Cambridge Core, October 12, 2016. https://www.cambridge.org/core/journals/ps-political-science-and-politics/article/abs/twitter-taunts-and-tirades-negative-campaigning-in-the-age-of-trump/D9EFBAABAE89FB0F64DD24B6DA049E89.

79. Drake, Bruce, and Jocelyn Kiley. "Americans Say the Nation's Political Debate Has Grown More Toxic and 'Heated' Rhetoric Could Lead to Violence." Pew Research Center, May 28, 2021. https://www.pewresearch.org/short-reads/2019/07/18/americans-say-the-nations-political-debate-has-grown-more-toxic-and-heated-rhetoric-could-lead-to-violence/.

80. Telonidis, Taki, and Brett Myers. "A Family Divided over Jan. 6: 'Traitors Get Shot.'" Reveal, January 17, 2023. https://revealnews.org/podcast/a-family-divided-over-jan-6-traitors-get-shot-2022/.

81. Brunier, Allison. "Covid-19 Pandemic Triggers 25% Increase in Prevalence of Anxiety and Depression Worldwide." World Health Organization. Accessed August 27, 2023. https://www.who.int/news/item/02-03-2022-covid-19-pandemic-triggers-25-increase-in-prevalence-of-anxiety-and-depression-worldwide.

82. Kozyrev, Anastasia, Sam Wineburg, Stephan Lewandowsky, and Ralph Hertwig. "Critical Ignoring as a Core Competence for Digital Citizens." ASSOCIATION FOR PSYCHOLOGICAL SCIENCE, 2023. DOI: 10.1177/09637214221121570 www.psychologicalscience.org/CDPS

83. Lewsey, Fred. "Slamming Political Rivals May Be the Most Effective Way to Go viralFred Lewsey." University of Cambridge, June 22, 2021. https://www.cam.ac.uk/stories/viralpolitics.

84. Murphy, Barbara E. "Remembering Nohemi Gonzalez, a Year Later." The New York Times, November 4, 2016. https://www.nytimes.com/2016/11/06/education/edlife/remembering-nohemi-gonzalez-a-year-later.html.

85. Johnson, Alex, and Raul A. Reyes. "Father of American Killed in Paris Attacks Sues Twitter, Facebook, Google." NBCNews.com, June 16, 2016. https://www.nbcnews.com/storyline/paris-terror-attacks/family-american-killed-paris-attacks-sues-twitter-facebook-google-n593351.

86. "Supreme Court Avoids Ruling on Law Shielding Social Media Companies." Spectrum News NY 1, May 18, 2023. https://ny1.com/nyc/all-boroughs/politics/2023/05/18/supreme-court-avoids-ruling-on-law-shielding-social-media-companies.

87. Silverman, Craig, Craig Timberg, Jeff Kao, and Jeremy B. Merrill. "Facebook Hosted Surge of Misinformation and Insurrection Threats in Months Leading up to Jan. 6 Attack, Records Show." ProPublica, January 4, 2022. https://www.propublica.org/article/facebook-hosted-surge-of-misinformation-and-insurrection-threats-in-months-leading-up-to-jan-6-attack-records-show.

88. Allyn, Bobby. "Here Are 4 Key Points from the Facebook Whistleblower's Testimony on Capitol Hill." NPR, October 6, 2021. https://www.npr.org/2021/10/05/1043377310/facebook-whistleblower-frances-haugen-congress.

89. Combs, Cory. "Council for Responsible Social Media Endorses Bipartisan Platform Accountability and Transparency Act." Issue One, July 6, 2023. https://issueone.org/press/council-for-responsible-social-media-endorses-bipartisan-platform-accountability-and-transparency-act/.

90. Ortutay, Barbara. "What You Should Know about Section 230, the Rule That Shaped Today's Internet." PBS, February 21, 2023. https://www.pbs.org/newshour/politics/what-you-should-know-about-section-230-the-rule-that-shaped-todays-internet#:~:text=That's%20thanks%20to%20Section%20230,by%20another%20information%20content%20provider.%E2%80%9D.

91. Contact your state senator here: https://www.senate.gov/general/contacting

92. Robertson, Dr Craig T. "Impartiality Unpacked: A Study of Four Countries." Reuters Institute for the Study of Journalism, June 23, 2021. https://reutersinstitute.politics.ox.ac.uk/digital-news-report/2021/impartiality-unpacked-study-four-countries.

93. Barrett et al., 2023

94. Hunt Allcott et al., "The Welfare Effects of Social Media," American Economic Review, March 2020, https://www.aeaweb.org/articles?id=10.1257%2Faer.20190658.

95. "Total Profit for Cable TV (Fox News, CNN and MSNBC)," Pew Research Center's Journalism Project, June 7, 2023, https://www.pewresearch.org/journalism/chart/sotnm-cable-total-profit-for-cable-tv/.

96. Walter, 24-25

97. "21 Findings from the Reuters Institute's Research in 2021 Still Relevant in 2022." Reuters Institute for the Study of Journalism, December 21, 2021. https://reutersinstitute.politics.ox.ac.uk/news/21-findings-reuters-institutes-research-2021-still-relevant-2022.

98. Watson, Amy. "Trust in News Media Worldwide 2023." Statista, June 14, 2023. https://www.statista.com/statistics/308468/importance-brand-journalist-creating-trust-news/.

99. Pickard, Victor, and Timothy Neff. "Op-Ed: Strengthen Our Democracy by Funding Public Media." Columbia Journalism Review, June 2, 2021. https://www.cjr.org/opinion/public-funding-media-democracy.php.

100. Lisa, Andrew. "32 Wildest Things Your Taxes Are Paying For." GOBankingRates, May 24, 2023. https://www.gobankingrates.com/taxes/tax-laws/shocking-things-taxes-pay-for/.

101. "[Vid] Why Public Media Isn't Propaganda (but Sometimes Is)." Spectacles Media, May 12, 2023. https://www.spectacles.news/public-media-and-propaganda/#fn1.

102. "Most Democratic Countries 2023." Wisevoter, May 2, 2023. https://wisevoter.com/country-rankings/most-democratic-countries/.

103. Fleck, Anna, and Felix Richter. "Infographic: The State of Democracy in the U.S." Statista Daily Data, July 4, 2022. https://www.statista.com/chart/27719/united-states-democracy-index/.

104. "Stress in America 2022: Concerned for the Future, Beset by Inflation." American Psychological Association, October 2022. https://www.apa.org/news/press/releases/stress/2022/concerned-future-inflation.

105. See more of Priscilla Shirer's wisdom on this page: https://quotlr.com/author/priscilla-shirer#google_vignette

106. Martin, Ryan. "Are Men Angrier than Women?" Psychology Today, June 21, 2021. https://www.psychologytoday.com/us/blog/all-the-rage/202106/are-men-angrier-women.

107. Linktree website: https://linktr.ee/evolutionrevolutionnow

108. Thompson, Erica. "Negotiation Expert Kwame Christian Is on a Mission to Change the World." The Columbus Dispatch, April 4, 2022. https://www.dispatch.com/story/business/2022/01/20/american-negotiation-institute-founder-kwame-christian-mission/8749470002/.

109. For more resources, guidance, and helpful worksheets, go to www.coachingforevolution.com

About the Author

Six-year-old Michael first learned about democracy and activism from his mother in 1972 while she was meeting with a Senator to fight for equal rights for women.

As he gazed upward in awe at the top of the State Capitol, he asked his mother, "who owns this beautiful home"? His mother squatted down, looked him in the eye and said, "the people do, but you have to fight for it sometimes".

She didn't know it yet, but that short conversation fueled the activist within him.

Mike earned early professional success as a Leadership and Development Coach and Master Trainer in the Tech field. He has a master's degree in leadership and is certified in NLP and Conflict Management. Mike has helped hundreds of clients improve their lives in his Conflict Transformation and Leadership Training Workshops.

He utilizes modern tools like chatbots and social learning in his workshops to help participants manage personal and team conflict.

He is a passionate advocate for helping our newest voting generations strengthen democracy. He volunteers at local charities and began a unique program that brings together Republicans and Democrats at food shelters to help them see each other as humans with a shared purpose.

His love of history led him to the new field of Revolution Science, which attempts to predict where revolutions and other political changes will occur in the world based upon elements that have appeared in other uprisings.

When Michael isn't writing, he spends time traveling the world with his wife and stubborn, but lovable, Jack Russell Terrier named Little Jack.

Connect with Mike:
Email: mikem@coachingforevolution.com
Website: CoachingforEvolution.com
Linktree: https://linktr.ee/evolutionrevolutionnow
Reddit: r/RevolutionWithoutTheR

www.ingramcontent.com/pod-product-compliance
Lightning Source LLC
Chambersburg PA
CBHW060226030426
42335CB00014B/1351

* 9 7 8 1 9 6 2 5 7 0 1 7 6 *